W9-AGU-762

Remembering Dale Earnhardt

By Rich Wolfe

If you have an interesting Dale Earnhardt story and would like to interview for possible inclusion in a reprint of the book, or if you have comments or suggestions, the author may be reached at:
EMAIL:poorfox@hotmail.com
www.gostealthisbook.com
www.ohwhataknight.com

ISBN: 0-9664912-2-X

EMAIL: poorfox@hotmail.com

Dedication

To the first annual reunion
of the Cape Cod Gang
in July, 2001.
Aging is a high price to pay for maturity.

Ralph Earnhardt, Dale's Dad.

Contents

Chat Rooms

Acknowledgements

Compiling the material for Remembering Dale Earnhardt has been an experience I shall never forget. During this difficult time, his friends and loved ones have opened their hearts to recall their personal experiences – the fun, excitement and interesting times spent with Dale Earnhardt.

I am grateful to the men and women who cooperated so willingly to make this tribute as special as it is. There is no family as close and wonderful as the NASCAR racing family.

I am blessed to have been allowed to be a part of it.

I am personally responsible for all errors, misstatements, inaccuracies, omissions, commissions, comminglings, communisms, fallacies. . . . If it's wrong and it's in this book, it's my fault.

My appreciation especially to Ellen, my Oklahoma typist, who can spell strange names, decipher garbled tapes, scribbled handwriting, and "unusual" editing marks and do this in a very quick and orderly fashion. Sincere thanks to the wonderful Heidi Day and the equally wondrous Dinah O'Brien in Scottsdale, Mr. Walter B. Planner, David Letterman and Kim Emmet at World Wide Pants, Eddy DeCock, Gene Cervelli, Kentucky Woman Special K, Jon Spoelstra and John Counsell (see ya in Lincoln in September), Ann Verhulst, Barbara Harris – the second smartest gal in Louisville, Tex Earnhardt, Gary Froid, Jackie Curry-Lynch, Mike Ambroziak, Pat Williams in Orlando, David Kindred, John Hargett, Rich McArdle, Carol "C. J." Carson, Mike Bynum, Joe Lettilier, Stan Baca, the oasis of NASCAR knowledge, Macmillan Publishing, Jay Brewer, Ashley Allen of *The Orlando Sentinel* and especially to Betty Carlan, of the International Motorsports Hall of Fame, who has kindly provided wonderful pictures that will help to make the book a special treasure to Dale Earnhardt fans.

Most of all, I want to thank Peter Golenbock for all his wonderful friendship and assistance on this project.

Lastly, a big thank you to Connie Goodman who was there from the beginning.

Preface

The sun came up this morning here in Kannapolis . . . over The Independent Tribune, the local newspaper that has used more than a few trees in reporting the exploits of their late hometown boy made good . . . a second later, over Studio One, the finest hotel in Dale Earnhardt's home town . . . and a second after that over Dale Earnhardt, Incorporated (DEI) – The Garage Mahal – up Highway 136, just before you get to Mooresville.

The sun wasn't nearly as bright – or so it seemed – three months earlier when their hero from, aptly named, Sedan Avenue, was laid to rest. He was a ninth-grade dropout who became King of the Hill in NASCAR circles. Harvard doesn't teach common sense, Yale doesn't have Perseverance 101, and the doctors at Johns Hopkins can't put a twinkle in your eyes. But Dale's dad, Ralph, who died unexpectedly in 1973, and his momma, Martha, managed to input all of the above in Dale while Ralph was carving out his own niche as one of stock car's all-time racing greats.

For years, there had been five sure things in North Carolina: The Tarheels going to the 'Dance,' Death, Taxes, Tobacco and Dale Earnhardt. Almost as sure a bet was Dale Earnhardt driving his pickup truck, and the fact that the pickup would be a mess.

Any boy growing up in rural America in the fifties was likely to have a fascination for stock cars. Earnhardt was raised in North Carolina near Highway 136. I was raised in the rural Midwest near a town called Lost Nation, on another Highway 136. Every Friday night in the summer, my dad and I would head to a town named Maquoketa, seventeen miles away, for the stock car races. Or Thursday and Sunday nights, he went to my older brothers' baseball games, but Friday night, we were at the Fairgrounds – just the two of us. Why, one Saturday night, he even took me to the much bigger races in the town of Farley. It was hard to believe that stock car racing could ever be bigger than Saturday night in Farley. . . .

Until many years later, when I went to the Coca Cola 600 at the Charlotte Motor Speedway in the early nineties. As a Sports Marketing Consultant, I spent considerable time perusing license plates at sporting events, which I did out of curiosity that day in Concord. What I saw blew me away: license plates from forty two states, a crowd far bigger than The Super Bowl, and more licensed driver and team merchandise than Mick Jagger ever dreamed about.

So, with my interest in racing rekindled, I made it to Indy for the first Brickyard 400 and have had wonderful times since at Bristol Saturday

Night – truly a sporting spectacle – Sears Point and Phoenix International Raceway.

Sadly, I missed Earnhardt winning the Brickyard in '95. Had tickets to the race, but it was raining so hard when we got to the Indianapolis Motor Speedway that, on the spur of the moment, we kept going two hundred forty miles west to a Cubs-Cardinals game in St. Louis. Halfway across Illinois, while flipping the radio dial, we heard an auto race being broadcast. Our worst fears were realized. Somehow, the Brickyard 400 was being run. Earnhardt was winning, and we weren't there.

Also, that same summer, I was in Indy working on a special golf tournament for then-governor Evan Bayh. I was staying at a beautiful hotel at Union Station in downtown Indianapolis called the Crown Plaza. The hotel has about six actual plush Pullman rail cars that are used as suites, and the General Manager, Bill Townsend, was kind enough to donate the use of the Diamond Jim Brady car for the Governor's cause.

While working one afternoon with the door open, I heard someone climbing the iron steps, and there appeared this beautiful young lady who asked if I minded her looking at the interior – like I was going to say 'no' to that request! It ended up being Betty Jo Yarborough, Cale's wife. They were in town for the Brickyard. So I'm looking at the poise, class and beauty of this woman, and I'm thinking "Well, ole Cale . . . he must have dumped his starter wife and married this young thing." At that point, Betty Jo remarked that she and Cale would be soon celebrating their thirty-second wedding anniversary – which proves my point that no area – and I mean 'no area' – of this country has prettier women than the South. If the Bishop had a church in the infield, he would kick out stained glass windows to get a closer look at those southern belles.

Why a book on Dale Earnhardt? Because I like him and wanted to know far more than his wins and trophies. Orthodox behavior has totally stifled creativity. Posturing and positioning one's image in order to maximize income has replaced honesty and bluntness. Political correctness has made phonies out of too many. Dale Earnhardt, who by basically being himself, beat the "prepackaged" boys at their own game.

For Dale Earnhardt and myself, and many like us, grew up in another time when Elvis was the King, Little Richard was the Queen, and Bruce Springsteen wasn't even in middle management yet. The people of our generation grew up at the very best time to be involved in sports: Baseball cards were collected, not for investments, but for the pure joy. You raced for the baseball diamond at every free moment to play until you were called home for supper – without an adult being anywhere in sight. A trip to a major league ballpark, if it happened, was magical. Double headers were plentiful. There were only eight teams in each baseball major league.

A trade was a major deal. There were no free agents. There were no agents. There was no Astroturf. There was no designated hitter. It was speed and control not velocity and location. It was the lane not the paint. There were no World Series night games. You waited impatiently each fall for the Converse Basketball Yearbook and every spring for the Louisville Slugger Handbook. It was a great time to grow up in America. And a weekend night at the race track with your dad was better than all this "touchy feely" crap some parents go for these days. Dale Earnhardt was a racer the way racers used to be in an America that is not the way it used to be.

From the age of ten, I have been a serious collector of sports books. During that time – for the sake of argument, let's call it thirty years – my favorite book style is the "eavesdropping" type where the subject talks in his own words without the "then he said" or "the air is so thick here you could cut it with a butter knife" waste of verbiage that makes it harder to get to the meat of the matter. Books like Lawrence Ritter's "The Glory of Their Times", Donald Honig's "Baseball When the Grass was Real", or any of my friend Pete Golenbock's books like "American Zoom" or "The Last Lap". Thus, I adopted that style when I started compiling oral histories of the Harry Carays of the world.

I'm a sports fan, first and foremost. This book is written solely for other sports fans. I really don't care what the publisher, editors or critics think. I'm only interested in the fans having an enjoyable read and getting their money's worth.

Thus, if a speaker rambles away from talking about Earnhardt and is digressing about something that most race fans would find interesting, it stays in the book. But if you find that I let them go on too far afield, and you have some good constructive criticism, feel free to jot it on the back of a twenty dollar bill and send it along.

It's amazing how many people – including myself – still refer to Dale Earnhardt in the present tense. Do you ever feel, like I do, that this is just an elaborate prank by Dale, and he's going to be there in the front row Sunday with that impish grin?

It's also interesting – as you will find in this book – how some people will view the same happening in completely different terms. Plus, with my format, you'll usually find that the most entertaining stories are from people you never heard of before.

In an effort to get more material into the book, the editor decided to merge certain paragraphs, leave out repetitive punctuation marks and omit some commas which will allow for the reader to receive an additional 20,000 words, the equivalent of 60 pages. More bang for your buck, more fodder for English teachers, less dead trees.

Dale Earnhardt was the King of the NASCAR Hill 76 times. Seventy-six hills make a pretty big mountain. So he became the King of the Mountain, and he liked the view . . . and we liked lookin' up at him.

Well, I gotta go now and get this book to the printer . . . in my pick-up truck with the mess in the front seat . . . and the sun will come up in the morning if the Lord's willin' and the creek don't rise.

Go now.

Rich Wolfe

Kannapolis, North Carolina
May 15, 2001

Chapter 1

David Letterman

John Boy and Billy

Jenna Fryer

Cale Yarborough

Humpy Wheeler

Chocolate Myers

Rick Sturtz

Ken Martin

Sam Bass

Betty Carlan

The Starting Grid

Dale Earnhardt at Age 4.

Wit Happens.

Late Night With David Letterman

Indianapolis native, David Letterman is a huge racing fan. Dale Earnhardt made several appearances on the show. On one appearance, Earnhardt told Letterman that he was the first man to win the Brickyard 400. Letterman responded "I thought Jeff Gordon won the first Brickyard 400 in 1994, and you won it in 1995." Earnhardt smiled impishly and said, "That's right. I'm the first man to win the Brickyard 400."

On February 16, 1998 shortly after winning his first and long-coveted Daytona 500, Dale Earnhardt appeared on Late Night with David Letterman to read his very own Top Ten List.

Reasons it Took Me 20 Years to Win the Daytona 500

10. It took me 19 years to realize I had the emergency brake on.

9. Finally rotated and balanced my mustache.

8. Quit training with the Canadian snowboarding team.

7. Stopped letting my 300+ pound cousin Ricky ride shotgun.

6. New strategy: pretend I'm Dave driving home on the Merritt Parkway.

5. Who cares that it took me 20 years - at least my name isn't Dick Trickle.

4. Just figured out that if you mash the gas pedal all the way down, the car takes off like a son of a b_tch.

3. My new pit crew - The Spice Girls.

2. This year whenever I passed somebody I gave them the finger.

1. My secret to success: one can of motor oil in my engine, one can of motor oil in my pants!

These Ten Things Are The Seven Signs You're Hooked on Earnhardt

John Boy and Billy

John Boy (From Graham, North Carolina) and Billy (From Gastonia, North Carolina) have ruled the Charlotte radio world from radio station WRFX in morning drive time for over 20 years. Their raucous, rockin' brand of fun times is now syndicated throughout North America and can be heard daily in more than a hundred markets.

In February, 1996 at Rockingham in the Goodwrench 400, with 50 miles to go and Bobby Hamilton leading, Earnhardt bumped Hamilton's Pontiac just enough to get it loose and take the lead. Earnhardt later blew by Dale Jarrett to win the race. Hamilton was furious. "I haven't won seven championships and I haven't won 60-some races but I'm smart enough to know ya don't do stuff like that this early in the season. That's an end-of-the-season move."

Dale Inman was in the observation tower that day spotting for Hamilton and was beside himself . . . and made no secret of his irritation towards Earnhardt. About a month later, Earnhardt approached Inman and said, "How much longer are you gonna be mad at me?" Inman said, "How much longer are you gonna be alive?"

Meantime, John Boy and Billy penned an up-tempo song played on their show that had everyone talking. As David Allan Coe would say, "We feel obliged to include it in this here book.":

There's a man in black his name is Dale
He's fast as lightning and mean as hell
He's not afraid to bump and grind
If it means he can leave your butt behind.

It's February in Rockingham
And that Goodwrench crew is ready to jam
As the number 'three moves through the field
Big Bobby Hamilton refuses to yield.

Coming out of turn four, what a sight to see
It was blue and red and Forty-three
But Earnhardt gave that Chevy the gas, and the 'three tried to pass
Petty said, "Hold on man." And Earnhardt said, "Watch this y'all."
Next thing ya know, the forty-three tagged the wall . . .

The man in black he flipped along
And drove as if he could do no wrong
Took the flag and pumped his fists
Petty's fans were really p_ssed.

The press caught Dale in Vict'ry Lane
And asked if he could please explain
"Well," Dale said, "I was racin' hard
I don't know what else to tell you, pard'."

All the crew at STP, was mad as mad could be
And lots of folks seemed surprised
That 'three car didn't get penalized
But NASCAR says it's just hard racing
And that's the kind of stuff you're facing.

I guess some guys have all the luck
And sometimes life just seems to suck

"After Earnhardt's death, we were so surprised. We knew, of course, that he was the man in NASCAR, but I had no idea it would be so worldwide or that it would be that much. I guess we had blinders. We know how it is around here. People actually, on the Sunday night of the accident, on the eleven o'clock news, people were going to the race shop and just standing out there kind of stunned. They were saying, "I don't even know why I'm here. I just felt like I needed to be somewhere.

We started talking racing back when everybody told us it wasn't going to happen because we were a rock and roll format – classic rock. What would happen, the guys at the shops would be listening to our morning show. I got to meet Barry Dodson, who is crew chief for Rusty Wallace, who won the championship in 1989. So the year before I got to be friends with Rusty and he would call in when he would win the races. After one time when Earnhardt won, he called in and said, "Can I get on this show? Or, is this just your boyfriends?" He called Rusty my boyfriend. "Can anybody – can the winner get on here? Or do you reserve it for your boyfriend? He didn't do too good yesterday."

We said, "Absolutely, Mr. Earnhardt." Then, from that it started like every time the guys would win, since those shops are mostly around here, the driver would call us on Monday morning to get on for bragging rights. So from that, it kind of snowballed to where even before we were syndicated we were on NASCAR's call list. It became official just from starting with Rusty and then Earnhardt.

When Earnhardt won his sixth championship, he called from the presidential suite of the Waldorf on the Friday morning before the ceremonies that weekend. He said, "They had to kick Hillary Clinton out of the room because she had come to New York to shop, and she always stays in the presidential suite. They kicked her out of the room and put me in it." They said all the Secret Service came in, there were gift baskets and everything left for the Earnhardts, and cleaned everything out before the Earnhardts checked in.

Earnhardt would never go for publicity, but if there was a kid, or somebody in a wheel chair, who would ask for him he would go for it. He didn't do it for the photo-op. In fact, a lot of times he would ask the media to leave if he was somewhere and they were getting ready to bring one of the kids in. He'd say, "Could you excuse us for just a second." And it would just be one on one.

The Talladega win where he came from so far behind was unbelievable. It was so interesting to hear him talk. Right before Daytona, he and Junior had just done the Corvette thing, and he was talking about how much he had enjoyed that. He said, "I love racing. I love doing it. I love watching it and hearing about it and learning new stuff and trying different things." He was still having a good time his entire life.

We did a promotion with him when we gave away a car from Earnhardt Chevrolet. We got to spend a lot of time there during the promo shoots with Dale and Teresa. We've seen him at different places like at the NASCAR Café. Richard Childress, the owner, has a farm right beside my wife's grandfather's farm right outside of Winston-Salem, North Carolina, in Welcome.

Around the race track, we would be standing there, and Earnhardt would come up and push you, "Get out of the way. We've got race drivers coming through." And stuff like that.

We always do our show down in Daytona the days leading up to the race. I remember early in the race when Tony Stewart had that wreck, I said, "Tony's going to walk away from that one." Then when Earnhardt wrecked, it didn't look that bad. You've seen Earnhardt climbing out of cars time and time again. You just expected him to. Then when he didn't, and when we saw Kenny Schrader come down the infield and saw his face, I knew it was bad then.

Our show is four hours long, going from 6:00 a.m. to 10:00 a.m. Eastern, Central 5 to 9 a.m. The next morning's show was hard. This is a comedy, light-hearted show with bits and characters and contests, and we just abandoned that. We opened up the phones and just let people talk.

We said, "We don't want to be at work this morning. I'm sure you don't. Imagine the guys, the racing family, nobody wants to come in, but we've got to be here. We have to deal with the grief." It really turned out to be probably one of the most talked-about shows that we've ever done. We're still getting poems, pictures, and songs. To this day, we're getting still probably about forty or fifty a week. People know how to get in touch with us and send stuff for us to forward to the Earnhardt family. Where they had photos – one guy had a photo of the lap before Earnhardt died. They are in the same corner. Look up there, and there was some figure. It was real blue sky, but it looked – my wife said that was an angel up there. And the next lap was where it hit. Stuff like that, with the cars all bunched up at the end. I've never seen so many grown men cry in my life. People tell us they appreciated the show. There's a guy who works at the station who grew up with Junior, and he was at the Earnhardt house that Monday night. He said that Teresa wanted to pass along how they appreciated the way we handled it. Instead of speculation of doing this or that, just opened it up and let everybody grieve. Just let them talk about their memories of him. That was very special.

That same morning, Travis Tritt called. He knew we were big Earnhardt fans, and so was he. He was in Nashville listening. He said, "Man, I remember being on my bus going somewhere and I pick up the phone. It's Dale Earnhardt. I thought it was a joke and said, "Sure, right." Dale said, "No, this is Dale Earnhardt, Travis."

Dale and Don Hawk, his business manager, were in their plane for the very first time, and Earnhardt took out a Travis Tritt song and said, "I want to play this song for you Don, and this is what it's all about." It was Travis' "I'm Gonna be Somebody." Dale played that and said, "That's it, Don." They were talking together about what they were going to do, and he said, "That's my song right there." Travis was relaying that story to us.

After that we were off the air. Don Hawk calls up. He said, "Man, I was listening to Travis tell that story. I remember it like it was yesterday. We were there." He went on, but he was broken up and crying and said he didn't want to be on the air but, "I just wanted to thank you because that just brought back memories."

The show just seemed to touch everybody. It's just unbelievable. I still can't believe it.

The only thing I've seen that was anything close to it was Elvis Presley in '77. Everybody was bowled over by that.

Most would say things like: "I just can't believe it." It's never going to be the same." "I don't know if I'm going to be able to go to a race without Earnhardt there." There were people crying, fond memories of chance meetings with him, lots of stories and just talking about him.

We were all excited. Michael Waltrip is a good friend of ours and we were waiting for him to win his first Cup race. I tell you that's the thing. That race went from Michael in Victory Lane with tears of joy to tears of sorrow in just a matter of minutes. We're still waiting for Michael to win another one because he wasn't going to call in that Monday morning and talk about his victory that he had been waiting for all these years.

We've had Michael on a whole bunch. We go back a pretty good ways. I'll tell you – that press conference they held at Daytona, Michael really helped me out. Just watching him at the press conference the way he handled himself. It was such a sudden thing. It was not like "Dale Earnhardt is sick." Or "Dale Earnhardt is hurt really bad." Then you almost can get a chance to mentally prepare yourself for the worst. The bad news came so fast that people were just floored by it.

At the end of the race, we'll never know if Earnhardt was blocking for Junior and Michael for his team? Earnhardt, if he had a pass, he would pass. He would win the Daytona 500 again. Maybe he didn't have it – you know, the car to pass them, and he was blocking. They were racing for position. That's something I'd always like to ask him, but nobody will ever know that.

I remember talking to Dale about him working in a service station when he wanted to race. There was an old junk car over there, and Ralph told him, "Aw, you can fix that one up and you can race that." Earnhardt got in it and wasn't doing too good. Ralph wrecked his car and made Dale stop so he could get in it and went and won the race with it.

Mail is still coming in. Not having him in a race does take something away because you don't get to 'beat the best' anymore.

The second Monday, we again had our Monday morning call from the winner.

One time we were supposed to go hunting with Dale. I went down to Hank Jones who used to handle his merchandise. He had a place in Orangeburg, South Carolina. I stayed there with him for a weekend and went hunting, but Earnhardt was doing something else, and he couldn't make it that weekend. I wish he had.

One time Dale came and hung around the radio station with us for about all morning. He had an Atlanta reporter with him from the Atlanta Journal. We always have food around. We were waiting to see the article, and when it came out it was like a paragraph. It was unbelievable. The reporter had been with Earnhardt all day and didn't have any more to say about it than that. NASCAR popularity has grown so much in recent years. I remember Dale Jarrett saying he went down to Atlanta and got on a radio show and the guys were floored by all the phone calls they got. HELLO – those idiots down there. That was at Atlanta. They don't realize what NASCAR was or all about. This was about ten years ago.

There would be a speedway at our home towns. We've really spent more time with Earnhardt, Jr. than we did Dale. He raced Legends cars. We've got a picture right here in the green room of Earnhardt, Jr. sitting beside his buds (John Boy and Billy), signed "Remember me, I wrecked your Legends car," Dale, Jr.

We have a race team. John Boy and Billy Racing has several cars in the Goodys Dash Series.

Earnhardt Flashes The Grin That Would Become Famous.

Furthermore, Officer, You and Earnhardt Were Tailgating!

Jenna Fryer

Jenna is an Associated Press Reporter based in Charlotte, North Carolina. Imagine doing nothing improper as you're driving and being pulled over by a state trooper and given a ticket . . . a ticket to a NASCAR race. Jenna Fryer had the unique experience of seeing this happen firsthand.

The first time I met Dale Earnhardt, it was a promotional event for Talladega – for the track. There was a breakfast in the morning and I was introduced to him. He kind of blew me off – like "Yeah, nice to meet you." I guess he forgot that I was a reporter because when I got in the state trooper's car, I was asking the police officer questions for my story, name, how did you get picked to do this, how did you guys get approval to do this? And I got about five questions into it, and Dale turns around and was like, "Are you a reporter?" I told him I was. He said, "I was wondering if you were qualified to ask questions like these." Dale rode in the passenger seat of a state trooper's car and they just kinda cruised up and down the highway and would pull over cars that were not doing anything wrong. The trooper would get the people out of the car. I think he then would say, "Well I'm going to have to give you a ticket." At that point, Dale would jump out of the police car and run up and hand them tickets to the race. I was in the car with them for a short while. They had a couple of cars following them – track personnel and things like that. And in the car they have a videographer from the track, and a track PR person. Because I was with Associated Press and shared my information with everyone, I got in the police car for a little while. I was in there as a reporter.

Earnhardt picked the people they pulled over. As I remember, the first vehicle they pulled over was a Ford truck. He chose that one because he drove Chevrolets. It was like, "Let's get this Ford." The driver of the Ford was just this nice man. He really wasn't sure who Dale Earnhardt was and wasn't a big racing fan. But he thanked them and had some people he could give the tickets to. The next car had a big '24' sticker on the back so Earnhardt thought they were Jeff Gordon fans so he picked them. They weren't Gordon fans. It was a local driver from Birmingham,

Alabama. They were big Earnhardt fans as well, and they just were falling all over themselves there on the side of the road. They were real excited. He stopped and let them take pictures. Because it was on the Interstate, it was actually in Hoover, Alabama, a suburb of Birmingham, cars would slow down 'cause everybody was like, "What's going on over there?" People as they were passing were recognizing it was Dale Earnhardt and he really slowed up traffic with all the commotion. Then the next car we pulled over had a Home Depot racing sticker on it, so he thought they were Tony Stewart fans, and it was just a worker at Home Depot. I think those were the only three stops when I was in the car.

This year in Winston-Salem at the annual NASCAR/Winston Cup preview, he didn't come to it. His son, Dale, Jr. told everybody the reason he wasn't there was because he had a piece of metal in his head since about 1977 that he was going to have removed the next day. Everybody wrote about it in the paper the next day – that he'd had this piece of metal. Now in hindsight, nobody thinks it was true. Seems like they just played around and told these stories so nobody really knew for sure.

I saw him about five more times since that first meeting in April of 2000. About a week or so after the promotion with the state troopers, he was testing at Talladega. It was the day Lee Petty had died. When he finally decided he would talk to the media, he came out and he leaned against the side of his car. The TV cameras crowded in around him asking about Lee Petty.

They had passed a rule that there would be a different size restrictor plate at Talladega that year. So I had legitimate questions I wanted to ask him about a news story. All the TV cameras being as annoying as they are just crowding around him, and I'm getting pushed closer and closer to him. Before I know it, I'm resting against the hood of his car, facing out. This circle is getting tighter and tighter and I'm getting squeezed in further and further. I could feel the sheet metal kind of crumpling under me. I guess he saw it, too, and he grabbed my arm and said, "Off the car, off the car," and he kind of yanked me off the car. I was a little bit upset about that.

Then a week later was the race, and it was qualifying. As he was coming off the track for qualifying, he pulled the car up and got out of the car and he was walking. I saw him, and said, "Can I ask you about your run?" He said, "Yes." So I had to walk with him and he put his arm around me as we walked. He answered all my questions and then right before he went off, he said, "Sorry I yelled at you last week."

I was at home when I heard he had died. I knew because of the interview Ken Schrader did on TV. I could tell with Ken's reaction. I kind of knew but was just waiting. The minute it was official, I had to go to the shop in Mooresville – The Garage Mahal – and start working. That was Sunday night, and all week I had to work because I'm based here in Charlotte. His shop's right up the road, so I was basically the main reporter on the story for the Associated Press. It wasn't until the Sunday that Rockingham was rained out, and I left the track that day and was in a restaurant with Brent, my husband. On their TV, they were showing the memorial service from Kannapolis, and it really hit me that he was dead. Because of my line of work, I was kept so busy working on it for a week, that it took a while to really register.

I was impressed with the race fans who went to his shop. They were just beside themselves, crying and leaving memorials. They lingered for a long time looking at the things people had left along the fence. It was kind of overwhelming. They reported that ten thousand people came on Monday alone, and it went on all week. None of these people knew him or met him but they were his fans. You realized just how many people really were touched by him, without really being touched by him at all.

My short description of Dale Earnhardt would be 'Crusty.' He told it like it was in a crusty kind of way. He told it like it was – scoffed at people who complained about the high speeds. He just told it like it was in his crusty little manner – blunt. I'm not saying that's not good. He was just himself, and his son is the same way. He's himself. They are who they are and they don't change for anyone.

The first few days following his death I was out at his shop. I was there to write about what was happening at the shop. I remember Sunday night when the word first got out, nothing had changed. But by the time I got out there Monday morning all the flags had been lowered to half-staff – the American flag, North Carolina flag, and the DEI flag. People had been leaving things. His race shop is called the Garage Mahal because it's so grand. I kind of remember that someone had tied balloons along the fence, and this lone black balloon broke free, and it was kind of floating off and you could see its reflection in the glass of the shop. There was a worker who had come outside to gather some of the things because there was a threat of rain. He saw it and ran after it and caught it and quietly tied it back on the fence. There was one guy there, 'Wild Bill' who was over seventy years old, and he rode his motorized scooter from somewhere in Kannapolis over to the garage to pay his respects. He had his dog on his lap, this little Lab dog, and the dog was wearing 'number three, Dale Earnhardt sunglasses and a little cap painted black with a little number 3 on it.' This old guy had known Dale's dad well. He rode all the way out there on his scooter with his little dog.

All those people quietly and humbly paying their respects . . . a very sad but amazing sight.

I'll Tell Ya How To Get Back On Your Feet: Miss A Couple Of Car Payments.

Cale Yarborough

Hall of Fame driver, Cale Yarborough is a successful car dealer in Florence, South Carolina

I used to race with Dale's dad, Ralph Earnhardt, in the early dirt track days on tracks all over the Carolinas. I've known Dale almost since he was born and watched him grow up and get started. I knew if he had any of his dad's genes in him, which he did, he would be a tremendous race car driver. His dad, Ralph, was a fierce competitor. When he showed up at the race track, you knew that if you won, you had your work cut out for you – that he was the man you'd have to beat. He raced primarily in Sportsman Division and on dirt tracks. He ran some Winston Cup races in his later years but didn't like it.

Dale was just a regular little kid. He was around the race tracks a lot and worked on his dad's car. He was just a regular little pit brat.

When Dale first came up in the early '70's, there was a guy in California named Rod Osterlund who came to me one day at the race track and says, "Cale, I'm going to make a change in my race team, and I'm going to put a driver in there. That driver I'm going to put in there is the person you tell me to put. It's that simple. Just tell me who you would recommend to drive my race car." Without a second thought, I said, "Dale Earnhardt." The rest is history.

At the time, I was winning everything there was to win so I guess that's why Osterlund came to me. I was never sorry I recommended him for that car. I was very proud when he won that first championship with Osterlund. That was one of the times I could say, "I told you so."

Dale Earnhardt was better than anybody else. He was competitive. Everybody knew right from the beginning where he was headed. At the beginning of his career he was involved in a lot of accidents, but most drivers who have that 'killer instinct' usually are involved in more than the normal amount of accidents.

Courtesy of Lowe's Motor Speedway

Earnhardt's An Itch
That Doesn't Go Away
With One Scratch.

Humpy Wheeler

Humpy Wheeler, president of the Charlotte Motor Speedway, has watched Dale Earnhardt race since Dale was running on the local Carolina dirt tracks as a boy. Wheeler, who began in racing as a promoter and who has gone on to become one of the pioneers and innovators in the sport, helped Dale get his foot in the door in Winston Cup racing. Wheeler recalls highlights of Earnhardt's long, glorious career.

D ale and I had been friends for over twenty years.
I would call him 'the last red-dirt racer' because that's the environment most all NASCAR was built on, and he's the last one of them – the last one to come out of that whole scene. This is the tradition of starting out on dirt tracks in small towns in the Carolinas, and moving up – never having enough money. Eking out a living. Doing it the really tough hard way. It's almost what made him one heck of a race driver. He learned to drive a loose race car on those dirt tracks. I watched him race on dirt many, many times. He was good, but he wasn't as great as he was in his prime years in NASCAR/Winston Cup racing. He wasn't as much of an intimidator. He was very young at that point, and there were a lot of guys who were the old hardened veterans who had been around a long time – they were the intimidators. He raced guys like Stick Elliott, Speedy Thompson, Mike Duvall, Billy Scott.

Even though he didn't have money, he was able to scrape enough together to put a car on the track. Dirt racing is more driver than car. On asphalt, you can't do that. He could take an average car and look great on dirt.

The one race that really sets him apart from anyone else was a hundred lap race they had at Metrolina Speedway in 1978, Labor Day weekend. He was driving for his former father-in-law, Robert Gee, who is Dale, Jr.'s grandfather. Rod Osterlund was at the track. I was there. It was the night following the Southern 500. Earnhardt started way back in the field at the Metrolina Speedway in Charlotte, a track with very narrow corners at that time. He just blasted his way up to the front and won the race with a few laps to go, against all these really good dirt-track drivers. That's where Osterlund really decided to get him to ride in the 300 mile at Charlotte. That's back when you could run a Winston Cup car on Saturday. He did well there. Then he put him in a Winston Cup car at Atlanta. And he put him on as his full-time driver the '79 season when he was Rookie of the Year, and he won a Championship in '80. That had never been done before.

In the early years, Dale was shy with the media. Remember that he came out of a cotton mill town where you're seen and not heard. He was just a very shy person. He was pretty introverted. He wasn't used to being in public. He was seen and not heard, as we say down here.

I think a combination of a lot of different people tried to help Dale at the beginning. We all saw that he had a lot of talent. I did some work with him. This would have been back in 1977. I've known him since he was a little boy 'cause his dad was a good friend of mine. We would talk a lot. He'd come to my office, and we'd have long conversations about racing and life and how you got to the top. Then we talked a lot about what you do when you get there and how to handle the press, how to handle NASCAR, those kinds of things. He was very independent. I could see that he was going to take some advice, but some of it he wasn't. But this was good because he's his own person, and that individuality is part of his charm, and you don't want to squash that. It's like people that tried to change Richard Petty when he was at the same stage. People loved him because of what he was like. What happened to Earnhardt is that he grew as a person – as he got more exposed but Ralph Seagraves and Wayne Robertson at R. J. Reynolds helped him a lot. We felt like he was going to go somewhere. We were all concerned about losing Richard Petty and David Pearson and Bobby Allison and Cale Yarborough – that's what was driving us back in those days. We knew they might be around but we knew that they wouldn't be winning races. He represented to us, back in the late '70's the new kid, particularly after he won a Rookie Championship. He wasn't The Intimidator then. He wasn't even close to being what he finally evolved into.

As a matter of fact, after he won a championship in 1980, he just wasn't prepared for that. The sport had gotten so much bigger. It certainly wasn't like winning the championships in 1975. R. J. Reynolds had gotten much more involved, particularly in the promotion of the champion. He just wasn't ready for it, and frankly most people aren't when they win it the first time. There are several reasons for that. One is the huge new demands on your time that didn't exist before. Racers are brought up in shops. Boxers are brought up gyms. Neither place is very social; you don't learn the social skills there. All of a sudden, you're the champion. You're thrust out into the world and have gone from the shop to the Waldorf. That's a pretty big jump to ask somebody to take. Versus that college football player who wins the Heisman award or goes on to be a pro. They've had a lot more training of the niceties of life. This was certainly not a plus. The other thing is he wasn't married at the time. I think most of us who have been around this thing a long time recognize the fact that your great race drivers, with very few exceptions, have pretty solid women behind them. You're always losing, and somebody has got to pick you up on Monday. You don't have a coach around. You don't have a trainer around you. The car owner's barking at you, the crew chief is thinking you're not pushing the throttle down hard enough or you're pushing it too hard. So the poor driver is sitting there without that cheerleader unless he's got that strong wife behind him, and he didn't have that at the time. He just didn't have the support system. His father wasn't there. So he did the best he could under the circumstances. You know it's just pretty unknown for a guy to win the Winston Cup Championship in his second full season, anyway. He had to get through that.

Then he had a pretty bad wreck at Pocono. That concerned me a great deal because he broke his collarbone and maybe a couple of ribs. He had to go to the hospital. You are always concerned with this. It's sort of like a boxer getting knocked out the first time. So what's he going to do next? Sometimes they fizzle out over a period of time. Drivers are like generals, they fade away; they don't go away real quick. He got through that okay.

I think things really started to change for him when he got married for the third time. This was to Teresa, and she had a very settling influence on him. He began to grow as a person, as a cause celebre so to speak, and he found out what so many celebrities find out – that's it's perfectly okay and even good to be yourself. The American public just might like you the way you are. I think most athletes don't think that 'cause they're used to watching movies and entertainers and singers that are all brought up or more-or-less geared toward celebrity. Athletes aren't. Once he got comfortable that he was his own person and that people still reacted favorably to him, he did better.

He began also to go through that stage where he became The Intimidator. He went from a 'wild man' to a guy that's going to win a lot of races to The Intimidator.

Early in his career, he was knocking a lot of walls down, as they say. Generally when people do that, you want to see them win a little bit, or you want to see them lead races, because if they're just knocking the wall down and not performing, you're going to mentally cast them aside. This is versus the guy who looks pretty good on the race track when he's not crashing.

You knew sooner or later, which he did, he'll become proficient. What he was so proficient at, he was able to go in the gray areas of the race track. I always say 'the areas where angels fear to tread.' Only the great race drivers can run there. He could do that and get away with it most of the time. No one can get away with it all of the time because these tracks, as big as they look, are very, very narrow places. If you get up in a helicopter at five thousand feet after the race is over, and look down at Charlotte, Atlanta or Daytona, you're looking down there and looking at a track that's really only about fifteen feet wide. You get out of that groove and you're probably going to wreck or you're going to burn your tires up and have problems that way.

I think 'total confidence' was the factor that caused Dale Earnhardt to go from winner to The Intimidator. You could see his confidence growing. He could do things with a car that he probably thought he couldn't do, although he never would admit that. He could get the car sideways and straighten it out and recover. You know, Allen Jones, the great Formula One racer once described stock car racing as a 'black art.' As Dale learned all the intricacies of what looks like a very simple thing – a stock car that turns left all the time, with fairly unsophisticated equipment under the skin, he began to understand the draft. He began to understand all the things that no one can explain about NASCAR racing and his confidence grew. Then he could do things to other drivers that he couldn't have gotten away with before.

Dale did become the racer that you either loved or you hated. You have to look at how the whole business was changing. It had gone from a working man's sport, very much like the NFL, to encompass other levels demographically. And part of that was younger, more affluent people, and also higher-class people, and the working people who Dale totally associated with, and who associated with him. And you had Darrell Waltrip, which appealed to maybe the more affluent. Then Jeff Gordon came along and had a great appeal to 'yuppies' and folks like that. It was totally along class lines. As a matter of fact we began to see that change in the social structure of who was coming to the races, by seeing the reaction toward him.

You could see evidence everywhere that Dale Earnhardt fans thought Dale could do no wrong. They stuck right to him. I think one of the best examples of that is the shrimp boat captains off the Carolinas coast. That's the primary fishing we have here, and it's a dying breed – very independent people. It's tough work, dirty, hot; it's the epitome of the working man. There's nothing fancy about a shrimp boat captain socially. I know a lot of these captains, and I never met one who wasn't an Earnhardt fan, who didn't feel Dale was their driver.

The people who work in the garages, or the people on all the docks feel the same way.

Jeff Gordon who came from California, probably could have driven Indy or Formula One, was the choice of the new yuppies and corporate vice presidents. He was their hero. He was the one they wanted associate with. He was the "Mod Squad" of the nineties. The way he dressed, the way he acted and the appeal that he had, the way he talked appealed to them. As they say down in the south, he was fancy.

I think deep down the people who booed Dale the worst had to at least respect the way he drove. They might not have respected it, but they had to acknowledge he was a good race driver. He was a great race driver.

I've talked about a lot of things with Dale. I don't know of anybody he talked to about intimidation, and the way he drove in that manner. He'd just say something about – if he'd been in a real intimidating posture somewhere with somebody he might say something, "Aw, he wouldn't get out of my way." Or something like that, he would joke about it. If you look at the pack in a race, there's a whole social structure in that pack. There's the bully, there's the good guy, there's the intense driver, there's the slick one that you never know what he's going to do – you don't trust, and there's the inexperienced one. It's a whole symphony of different mentalities and psyches that are operating in that whole thing. What kind of personality that you have in a race car and a pack draft is to a great extent going to mean how many races you are going to win. The over-reactors may be good race drivers, but they're not going to win a whole lot of races because they are going to take too much emotion into it. Dale recognized all that. He was the guy on the interstate in the big black Suburban a foot off your bumper. Most people moved over, or got mad, or wanted to slam the brakes on, but they didn't want the Suburban coming up into the rear seat either.

Dale's career turned in a little bit of a different direction when he had that bad wreck at Talladega. He had won a few championships already. It was a wreck that insiders have said many times was not a survivable wreck. Getting hit on a super-speedway, Daytona or Talladega speedway in the top while you're upside down – was not a survivable wreck. Dale had already been through the bad part when he hit the wall and the car flipped several times. What a lot of people don't know is – he told me several months afterward that he could see the car coming at him while he was sitting there. That's something you would never forget because at that point, he didn't say this to me, but you might be saying, "This is it." I don't even remember who was the driver of the car that plowed into him, but it would be in the tape. The incredible thing is that despite the broken sternum and ribs and everything else that happened is that – adrenalin is what caused this – he got out of the car and walked to the ambulance. That's got to be one of the great things in the sport because everybody on pit row thought he was dead. It was right in front of all of them.

He made an amazing comeback the next week. He won the pole at Watkins Glen. Then after that he went to Indianapolis, and things started going downhill after that. I think all of it caught up with him. Obviously he had a lot of healing to do. But he was getting on with his career. Very few guys win races after they are forty-five years old. The list is pretty small. He was thinking about that. He actually, I think at the Talladega race, had already won his seven championships. He had done all that. Of course, he desperately, really wanted to win that eighth one and beat Richard Petty. He really started questioning himself – whether it was him or the car. That's the age-old problem – "Is it me or the car?" You start seeing drivers do that later on in their career, particularly after they've been in a pretty horrific accident. He had made a lot of money. The thing that made it difficult for him was – "What am I going to do?" At that time he hadn't built that monstrous shop and he didn't have his race teams. He was still in essence working for Richard Childress.

Again, if the pressure of winning one championship is tough, what is it like to have to go through all seven. Because when you win the championship, there's just some unwritten law in racing that you devote your spare time in that year that follows representing the sport. Some of them are not as active as others, but even the ones who aren't active, it is still a tremendous time commitment for them. It's very wearing.

Being a race driver is just like being in a herd of antelope on the plain. As soon as you get a little bit weak, the lion comes after you. People were really beginning to say he'd lost it, that his ability was gone, and that he'd never win another race. That goes back to what I said about fading away, that's usually what happens to guys. They just stop winning. So Dale went through that period for about eighteen months to two years. Things weren't good. Then he made an amazing comeback by winning the Daytona 500. Not only that, he started running up in the top five again. And actually he came back and won a short track race at Bristol.

We definitely saw that at least a good part of him had come back, certainly not the Earnhardt that was in his prime, but his fans got charged up again. Then he built that monstrous place outside of Mooresville. The thing that also helped recharge him was Junior coming along. Although Junior had done fairly well in short track racing, you never know what a guy is going to do until he gets in a Busch car – it's hard to look good in a Busch car. So what's he going to do? The car was underpowered and you don't see the domination in Busch racing that you sometimes do in Winston Cup. When he did well in Busch, and then moved up to Winston Cup, and then he won Texas, I think that was a milestone in Dale, Sr.'s life. We all, to a certain extent, live through our children.

Dale's father, Ralph, had never really gotten to see Dale perform, because I think Dale was twenty two years old when his father died suddenly at the age of forty five. He had seen him on some dirt tracks but he hadn't really seen him do what he really wanted to do. Dale's father had a tremendous influence on him.

There was some irony in the Daytona race – certainly no one had been killed there a half second from the finish line.

I don't think Dale Earnhardt would have raced a whole lot longer – maybe two or three years. He didn't want to fade away. At the same time, it's like the Emmy Lou Harris song, the fighter still remains, whether it's the shell or not. That's the tough part. That would have been the tough thing for him to figure out. Where is that point?

We did not know the depth that this sport had reached until Dale died. That's a terrible way to find out about it. I would never have thought that I would see a race driver of any kind on the cover of Time magazine.

Earnhardt Drove So Chocolate Could Save His Hands For Surgery.

Chocolate Myers

Danny "Chocolate" Myers is the son of legendary race car driver Bobby Myers, who was killed in a crash in the Southern 500 at Darlington in September of 1957. Myers, a bulking man with a bushy black beard, grew up with team owner Richard Childress and has been a mechanic and gas man for the Goodwrench team since 1983. He acted as an unofficial body guard for Dale Earnhardt when they were together.

Idon't know whether or not I was a 'protector' for Dale Earnhardt, but in the early days when we were racing and winning, he was The Intimidator, I guess that, when the race was over, I was always at the car and was always with him. It wasn't just me; we all were Dale Earnhardt's protectors. We loved him. He was our driver. We'd probably do anything for him.

Most of Dale's and my relationship was spent at the track, and it was mostly business. But when we did have a chance to fly on the plane to the race track, from the race track, we'd have a chance to go to the farm, to go fishing, to do a few things with Dale. When we did, he was a totally different person. He was so intense. When he was at the race track, when he walked in the gate at the race track, he had people pulling on him from every direction. I had often thought about how tough it must have been for him. When he was at the race track, he couldn't even come out of the truck. If he walked from the truck to the car, just a few feet, he had a crowd with him. I'm sure it was aggravating sometimes and it was hard on him to concentrate on what he had to do. But yet when we got on the plane, or when we went to the farm, he was a different guy. He was a family guy. He loved his family. We had times to talk before about his relationship with his dad and what his dad taught him.

He was just a unique guy. He was a racer – that's all he wanted to do. He was the best, and I'm sure everybody has told you that. But I knew Dale Earnhardt was going to be the best that ever was a long time before anybody realized it.

For a while there, it seemed he was doing something incredible every week. I guess the 'Pass in the Grass' – that's a move that will live forever probably. Driving on the grass at high speeds is extremely dangerous. You see guys going across the grass slow and spinning out. He went across the grass, and I'm not talking about across the edge of the grass, he was really in the grass, and come across it, and come out with the lead and never checked up.

That's just one of them. There are so many. We were at Charlotte years ago. We were running. We were decent, but weren't going to win the race. We weren't going to be a contender to win the race. The 'caution' comes out right at the end of the race, with only a few laps to go. When it goes back to green, there's only going to be three or four laps. That's all that will be left. I told Dale to stay out, and we would ride it out, and we'd get us a decent, top ten, finish out of it. We were probably sixth or seventh at the time. About that time, Earnhardt came back on the radio and said, "Boys, I'm coming down pit road. Put me four tires on here. I didn't come down here to finish in the top ten. I come down here to win this race." Earnhardt came in, and we put him four tires on, and I think we finished second that day. You didn't have to watch the race to know that Earnhardt was doing something because you could just sit and watch the grandstands and you could see people standing up and pointing, and you knew it was him. He was just that good.

Dale was an inspiration to the people on the Goodwrench team. When you've got somebody like Dale Earnhardt driving the car and another guy like Richard Childress as the team owner, and you don't give everything you've got, then you'd just feel so bad about it, because you know these guys are giving their part. That's what I've told people before. When you don't give it your all, you're not only letting yourself down, you're letting everybody down. I think that's what made this team so successful because of those two guys giving it the dedication that they did, and then we all fell right in there with them.

A couple of years ago, Dale was hurt from the crash and from the years of driving, and we were off, and we weren't running good and people had counted us out. Probably some of the guys on the team thought maybe we were still doing the same things we'd been doing and things just weren't coming together. Before we went to the 2000 Daytona, Dale had the surgery, had his neck and back fixed. Then, my gosh, it was just like he was there. He was better. He was great. He was the old Earnhardt.

This year we had our company Christmas party. I wore a tux. It wasn't formal, but I wore my tux. Earnhardt said, "Chocolate, why are you wearing your tux?" I said, "Dale, I bought this thing to wear back to New York." He said, "Well you don't worry about it. We're going back to New York 'cause we're going to win this championship." He knew that he could do it. He assured us that we all could do it together. That was the plan. I just feel like it was there, and this was going to be the year we would do it again. We almost did it last year. We were so close. We just had a few bad things happen to us, or we could have been a contender right down to the wire. Dale Earnhardt, with the seven championships he has got, it's seven of them – it could have been ten or twelve just as easy. He was that good. And he was good everywhere we went. You've got some guys who are good at a Speedway. You've got some guys who are good at a road course. You've got some guys who are good at a short track. Dale was good everywhere we went.

This is my life. I'm here with Richard Childress' racing. I hope I'm here till I can't go anymore. This is what we do. We've got to continue doing this even though it's tough sometimes. It's tough when we go back to somewhere where we've got a special feeling. And you do get choked up, but we've got to carry on. We've talked about it before. If something happened to any of us, what are we going to do? We're going to keep going. That's what we do. Every once in a while, I'll have one of those moments and get a lump in my throat. I think about it quite often. We went to Martinsville recently. Everything was good. We were driving to the race track, and I see the GM Goodwrench Service Plus souvenir trailer. It looks kind of different, but I couldn't see it clearly. It's the first time I had been close to it. It had, from top to bottom, from front to rear, notes to Dale that people had written and signed. It just choked me up.

We came through this tragedy at Daytona. We don't know what's going to happen. We put Kevin Harvick in the car, and three races later we win a race. To win that race was, for me personally, great. How great it is that we're winning races with this new guy, this kid, and how proud Dale would be if he could see it. I've never had emotions like that so – both ways. We all thought about it. We knew that was God's will. You could not have planned that. You couldn't have written a script. The chances of that happening were pretty phenomenal.

When the race was over, I think we were all so emotional that we just didn't say anything. Everybody there, not only the guys on this race team, but the guys on the other race teams, and the people in the stands, all had a special feeling. It was just tremendous.

I'm just so proud to have been a part of it. It was good from the very first to the bitter end. It was good times. I think that Richard Childress and Dale Earnhardt were just such a great combination of owner/driver that the rest of it just fell in place with the guys we had. We were all dedicated to those guys.

Diane Fair, Cumberland Times

Rick Sturtz (see next story) sits in his Dale Earnhart Signature Series Silverado.

Rick Won A Million Bucks. Big Deal. I'm Workin' On My Second Million–I Gave Up On My First.

Rick Sturtz

Rick is from Northern Maryland. He won the Winston No-Bull Five, a contest sponsored by the R. J. Reynolds Company. Rick "won the lottery" twice: He got to meet his look-alike idol and won a million dollars on the same weekend . . . . and it couldn't have happened to a nicer guy.

I've been an Earnhardt fan for longer than twenty years. I began following him when he first started driving the Wrangler car. A lot of people say I look like him, but that wasn't why I started rooting for him. It was just his style of driving – he was aggressive and I like that. It was just fun watching him go from the rear to the front. The race when I won he made up from eighteenth place in five laps. Of all the races I've ever seen him win, that was probably one of the best ones I've seen. It was amazing.

In 1993, I bought him a limited edition hunting knife and lighter that said Zippo (they only made about 500 of them here in Pennsylvania) as a birthday present and thought I was going to get to give it to him, but I didn't. I never got to catch up with him. I actually got to give it to him but it was after the Talladega race when we went back down to his dealership in North Carolina. The way he is, some days he likes to be around the fans and others not. I guess he has good and bad days like everyone else.

I had filled out a form in May at the Coca Cola 600 last spring in Charlotte. They give you a free carton of cigarettes. That application you fill out is what they use as a contest entry – send it to a sweepstakes place in Minnesota where the names are actually drawn. I had no idea I'd ever be drawn, but that's how it all started – just signing up for a carton of cigarettes. We go to a lot of races, and I do have a bad habit of smoking so to get a free carton of cigarettes, I just signed my name, and then just forgot about it.

Then in September, a Federal Express driver came up to my garage and had an envelope for me that I had to sign for. So I signed for it, and said, "Is it a check?" He said, "I have no idea what it is."

I went inside and opened it. My wife was at work. It said I was chosen as a contestant for the Winston No-Bull Five contest which I figured was just a bunch of bull to begin with because how many times does this happen to someone like me. In order to be eligible for it, I had to have the papers signed and notarized and returned by a certain date. When my wife came home, we read over them and took them to an accountant. He told us just to sign, get it notarized and send it back in. It wasn't long after that a guy named Mark Rogers with R. J. Reynolds called and said he received the papers we had notarized. He told us he would send plane tickets out to go to the October, 2000, Talladega race. The papers listed the names of the five drivers who were in the contest and said we had a chance to win a million dollars if the driver we were paired up with actually won the race. They sent us the plane tickets and we flew down to Birmingham, Alabama. This was all very exciting. We had never been in a stretch limo before. The R. J. Reynolds tobacco people have got to be the greatest people I've ever met. The Wynfrey hotel they put us in was great. They waited on us hand and foot; we didn't have to do anything. It was just unreal. The most exciting part was when we got to Alpine, Alabama and Dale Earnhardt flew in on his helicopter and we got to meet him right there. That was when it really began to sink in. Two stretch limos picked us up at the airport and they drove us to a place called Alpine, Alabama. It was like a hunting club. They had the five drivers come in and they had a skeet shoot. This was at nighttime. They had like twenty shots at twenty clay pigeons and how many targets they actually hit were how they were rated – one through five. They had the contestants' names on the right side of the board but they were covered up so we had no idea where we were. So when they shot, Earnhardt finished fourth and when they unveiled the names, my name was beside his. My legs went weak.

They had a picnic for us there. We were sitting there eating and then walked down to where they were going to have the skeet shoot. There was a fence around it, but the guy from R. J. Reynolds said we could go in. The fence was just to keep the public out. Karen and I were getting ready to sit down, and Dale was standing up by the fence. Karen, my wife, says, "Hey Dale, come here a minute." He started walking over, and I said, "Karen, I can't believe you did that." He came over and that was where the friendship began. When we shook hands, it was like we had known each other for life. I told him I was a fan of his for a long time.

Actually I didn't know my name was beside Earnhardt's because I was walking around. Karen came up and said, "You aren't going to believe who they paired you up with." I said, "Who?" She said, "No, take a guess." I said, "No, just tell me." She said, "Dale Earnhardt." I talked to him then and we had pictures taken on a stage there. Jeff Gordon and he were standing there talking, and I was standing beside Dale. Jeff Gordon said, "Dale, I didn't know you had another brother." We didn't only get to meet Dale, but we met Jeff Gordon, Steve Park, and Mark Martin.

I'm a nobody, and it was just unreal how they stood and talked to me like I had been their friend for a long time. When have you ever heard of a NASCAR driver getting in trouble for drinking and driving, or drugs or anything like that? You don't hear about that in NASCAR. This was on a Thursday and the race wasn't until Sunday.

On Friday they had a thing at the track for us. Tom T. Hall and his band were there. They asked us to get up on the stage and sing, "Ride, Sally, Ride," in front of all these NASCAR fans. That was embarrassing; I'm not used to facing a bunch of people like that. All these NASCAR fans were drinking and about half crazy and it was just unreal. I think Karen rolled on the ground laughing.

On Saturday they got us up early and we out to eat and then took us to the Busch race. We were up in the stands. It was a really hot day. Here came Mark Rogers and said, "Come on guys, we're going to go over in the suites and sit." So they took us out of the stands and into the air-conditioned suites and that's where we watched the race from. It was unreal.

Sunday morning we had to get up early. We all had garage and pit passes to go in to actually where they inspect the cars and everything. I had been in the pits before but had never had a garage pass. I knew they went over the cars with a fine-tooth comb to inspect them and make sure they are legal and everything is up to snuff. They were pulling the coil springs out of them and it was just unbelievable the things they have to do to those cars before they let the guys drive them. Even my wife was amazed and she's not mechanically inclined or anything. She was just totally amazed at all the things they do.

I was so happy at this point. If Earnhardt had not won the race, I wouldn't have won any money. But they could have sent me home before the race, and I still would have been the happiest guy in the world.

Before the race even started, we met with Richard Childress and he actually signed the shirt I had on that day. He said, "Rick, you and your wife are going to go home with some money today." Dale even told me that before the race started. He said, "Rick, we're going to get that money."

There was real incentive for the drivers, too. They got a million dollar bonus if they won.

I was so wired up thinking about everything that I didn't sleep the whole time I was there. I really was thinking about the money because all the five contestants had made a pact. We said whoever won would give each of the other four ten thousand dollars. The photographer, Bryan

Snipes, had a digital camera and he showed us pictures he had taken during the day. While we were looking at them and realized how much fun we were having, we thought it would be fun to do that so that each person would go home with more than just having won the trip. We were talking; first they were talking twenty five thousand dollars apiece. One couple from Illinois decided against it 'cause they thought it was too much. Tim Reynolds suggested we just go ten thousand, and everybody agreed on that. When we got our money, I sent each of the other contestants ten thousand dollars apiece. It was in the newspaper when we first did it but I don't think many knew about it.

It's impossible to describe what we were feeling. I knew we would be able to pay off all our bills, and pay off the house and pay off the little garage I have here. We would buy some things we weren't able to afford before. We wanted to help some charities out and our kids. I just had a feeling. I told Mark Rogers all day long that Dale was going to win it.

Karen told me not to hold my breath.

They put us in the stands where they had closed circuit TV's 'cause we couldn't see the whole race track. We had real nice chairs and were able to see the entire race on the televisions. There was food and drinks there for us. Halfway through the race, the other contestants kept saying, Earnhardt's going to win this race, and Rick's going to go home with this money. I said, "You don't know that; they've still got a hundred laps to go. You can't judge like that." Earnhardt didn't start well. I was still telling Mark Rogers he was going to win it, but Mark said, "I don't know Rick. Look where he's at." I said, "I don't care Mark. I'm not going to lose my faith; he's going to win this race." I think with five laps to go, he was running eighteenth. He kept saying, "Rick, it don't look good." I said, "Mark, he's going to do it." On the last two laps, he started forging forward. The rest of it is history. He crossed that finish line and got the checkered flag.

I really thought he had a shot. On the last lap, he was still in the lead. I think Nemechek was coming up through the center of the pack. I could see when they came into turn three that he was still in the lead. The crowd, the fans, just went crazy. Everybody stood up and screamed and hollered. Karen was jumping up and down. It was probably the greatest comeback he ever had – might be the greatest race he ever had. I didn't get to see a lot of them on TV but that was the best one I'd ever seen.

I went into hysteria. I hugged Mark Rogers and couldn't quit thanking him. I hugged and kissed my wife. By that time, Richard Sanders, President of Sports Marketing for R. J. Reynolds had us brought to the winner's circle. Here comes Dale in. They started throwing all this confetti all over the place. The next thing I knew, Richard Sanders was helping me up on the car, and Dale reaches down and pulls me up on the car.

It was so unreal. My legs were so weak. It was indescribable.

The fact that I had actually won a million dollars never even sunk in until a month after Christmas. I was there in the winner's circle and was on top of the car. We got down off the car and my wife was hugging Teresa, Dale's wife. I told Teresa, "You've got to be married to the greatest guy in the world." He hugged me, and I hugged him. He was actually telling me what I should do with my money. He said, "Take that money, Rick, and invest it wisely. Take it easy." It was just unreal. I did everything he told me to do. He must have known how I was used to working seven days a week and 12 – 16 hours a day, and I just had a deep feeling these guys knew what we did before we actually went on this trip. How else would he know, unless they talked to my wife when I wasn't around or something? But he just knew stuff about me. He could have seen my hands – 'cause I've got calluses on my hands you wouldn't believe, and cuts and bruises 'cause actually I'm a mechanic by trade but I drove a truck for a lot of years. That's very possible the guy could see – 'cause you can tell a guy who does get out and get his hands greasy compared to somebody who does office work and stuff like that. There's a big difference.

We were probably in the winner's circle for about 45 minutes. We talked, and they took picture after picture after picture. We actually helped him hold up the million-dollar check. I don't even know what I was thinking there. I'd really like to remember but then again I don't want to remember.

Then a guy from R. J. Reynolds took us to the pressroom where they were interviewing Joe Nemechek, and I was next. They put me on a stool. I don't know if they had me on TV or what, but they interviewed me – asked me what I was going to do with my money, and if I was going to continue working, and all kinds of questions. They asked me if I knew Dale Earnhardt from before. I said, "I've known his name for probably twenty years, but this is the first time I've actually gotten to meet him and be with him." There were just all kinds of questions.

Actually I got to meet Mike Helton, President of NASCAR. There were a lot of big shots there.

The others – the ones who did not win the million – were sitting in the limo over on the track when I passed them at the airport exit to go back to the Hotel. They couldn't leave until they were finished interviewing me. They said, They thought I was never going to shut up. I said, "Well, I wasn't gone that long." Those people were so happy for us, and I told them that if I hadn't won, I would be just as happy for them.

They actually took us out to dinner. You wouldn't believe this place; I can't remember the name of it, but there were gigantic palm trees inside this restaurant. They had big long tables there. There was a stream of water running down behind us that had gold fish in it that must have been twelve inches long. They were just swimming up the stream in this restaurant where they took us. I guess that was a goodbye dinner because after we finished they took us back to the hotel, and we had to get up a six o'clock the next morning to catch the flight home. We didn't sleep much that night.

After we got back to the Hotel on Sunday evening, I called to tell my mom, but she already had seen it on TV so she knew it. I can't even remember anything she said. I told her I loved her, and we were on our way home. Everybody was just so happy. I've got four brothers. When I got home, they were over at an outdoor sportsmen's club up here right above where I live. They said just about everybody in the club just started breaking down with tears when they saw Earnhardt pull me up on that car.

On the Monday we got back from Talladega, we had 105 calls that evening. We had about 89 on Tuesday. Eighty-something on Wednesday, but then it started decreasing. Nobody wanted anything. They just called to thank us and didn't mention the money at all. I have a small garage here and it's a good business.

We got back home and my house and garage were just totally decorated. They wrote one million dollars across my garage. There were umpteen amount of people just waiting here and the Cumberland Times, the local newspaper, was here. It was like a welcome home party – a wonderful dream that wasn't going to end. Actually coming home on the plane, my wife said, "We're just sleeping, and we're going to wake up and find out that was a dream." I said, "No, Karen, I think it's for real."

I actually ordered the new Silverado on Monday when we got back from Talladega. We got home Monday evening. A lady from the Benny Parsons show called and asked if they called back at 8:30, would I be willing to talk. I said, "Yeah, no problem." They called back and I got on the air. They said Dale was there, and I was talking to them. Benny said, "What about this truck?" Dale must have known about the truck before 'cause I told Richard Sanders about it. I told Dale, "Dale, a black Signature Series Silverado would certainly look good in my garage." He said, "Rick you don't want that truck. Invest your money." I said, "No, Dale, I'd really like to have that truck." He said, "Well, I'll take care of it." Two weeks later Tom Johnston, general manager of Dale Earnhardt Chevrolet in Newton, North Carolina called and said my truck was ready. I was surprised that it happened so fast, but I told him, "I'm on my way down." We left on a Sunday and got a motel in Mooresville and then we got on Interstate 41 to Newton, North Carolina, where we met Tom Johnston. He showed us this truck. It was just unreal; it even had Dale's signature there on the dash. It was the truck I always had in mind but we could never afford to buy. The day before we went down, they took it to Dale's DEI over in Mooresville and that's where Dale actually sat in the passenger side and signed the dash. They told me it wouldn't come off, so I've Armor-All-ed the dash and everything so it must be some kind of special marker. There's Goodwrench racing on the hood and on the sides. This is a 2001 Silverado Limited Edition, Dale Earnhardt Signature Series pickup truck.

On Monday when we came to the motel back from Newton from looking at this pickup truck, we called Dale Earnhardt's place and told him we were in town and wanted to talk to him. Well, "Come on down. You're more than welcome." It was just unreal. So about 11:00 or 11:30, we arrived at Dale's place and we had to go upstairs. We stood in front of this camera, and they asked our names. We told them and were let into an elevator. It was immaculate – lined with leather. So we get upstairs and the lady told us to have a seat and Dale would be right with us. We were sitting there in this unbelievable building of his, and here he comes walking around the corner. I stood up and shook his hand. Karen stood up to shake his hand, and he said, "I don't want to shake your hand, I want a hug." He gave her a great big hug. He said, "Come on and walk with me. I've got to take this car over to get the interior redone. I want you guys to walk around, make yourself at home, and I'll be right back and we'll have lunch together." It was like a dream. We were actually going to have lunch with Dale Earnhardt.

While we were waiting, Dale's brother Randy took us all through his shop.

After he came back, we went into his dining room. We go through this line and get what we want to eat. I think I had some kind of chicken and then we sat down. Here came Dale's mother, Dale's wife Teresa, Dale, Jr. Kerry, Kelly and her new baby, Michael Waltrip, Brian and others I can't even remember. When we started to eat, Dale went up into the room there where he must have had a video of the race, and he plays the race over. He kept asking questions, "Where do you think your horse is going to finish?" I said, "You're going to win it." We watched the race and it was just unreal.

After that we went to R. J. Reynolds in Winston-Salem. We went in and talked to photographer Bryan Snipes. We spent some time with Mark Rogers, thanking him. Then we went to see Richard Sanders and thanked him. He couldn't believe it. The way I understand it is we're the only ones who ever went back to thank those people for what they did for us. They were so great to us. We called them and actually Richard Sanders gave us tickets to go to Rockingham this year. We went down there the week after Dale's accident. I wish we hadn't gone because the race was not the same without Dale being there.

In February, I was in my living room sitting on the sofa watching the Daytona 500. When Dale wrecked, I was concerned, but I said, "He'll just shake it off." I kept watching for him to climb out of the car but he never climbed out. When Kenny Schrader went over to the car and motioned for help, I said to Karen, "Something's wrong. He must be hurt." We never thought he was going to pass away. About an hour later my aunt called and she said, "Richard, I just found on the internet that Dale has passed away." I said, "No way. There's no way it could get on the computer that fast." She said, "Yes, it is, and it's coming on TV." Karen turned the TV back on and that's when Mike Helton announced that Dale had passed away.

After his death, I read all the stories about him. As much as I thought I knew about Dale Earnhardt, there was so much charity work that he did that people didn't know about

This is really hard. I lost not only my favorite driver, but also a neat friend. We had plans to go hunting at some time in the future. While we were in the winner's circle, I said, "Dale I would really like to go hunting with you." He said we would do that. Brian said, "If he told you he was going to take you hunting, he will definitely take you hunting." I am into about the same type of stuff he was into – hunting and fishing. I can tell you right now I don't like baseball or football or golf. NASCAR and hunting are the two things I always did.

At Rockingham, it was hard because they had a big memorial in front at a place that's called 'The Rock.' People had just put all kinds of things that they actually wrote to Dale. It was very hard.

At home, all my friends were tickled pink about what had happened to me. We called Richard Sanders and he said, "Well, you just go to 'will call' and your tickets will be there; it won't cost you a thing. We went to the Winston tractor/trailer and told them what we were doing. The R. J. Reynolds' guy knew who we were. I said, "We've got some tickets here that Richard Sanders put away for us." We started walking away, and he told us where to go. He said, "Hold on sir." He called for a golf cart and said, "We're going to take you to get your tickets and take you to your seats." Instead of us having to walk, he put us in a golf cart and took us to our seats.

I've never met people who were as nice to me as the R. J. Reynolds people actually have been. It's so hard to describe.

Since October, it's been fantastic, up until February. Then it took a turn for the worse for a week or so. Once we got to Rockingham and saw that race which I didn't enjoy real well because Dale wasn't there, but we talked to Richard Childress and went to Welcome, North Carolina and talked to Kevin Hammond and some guys and Chocolate Myers. Like I told Kevin Hammond, I said, "Kevin, everybody misses him. If it would bring Dale back, I'd give the million dollars back. It wouldn't be a problem at all."

One thing I have done since winning the money, I have quite a bit of Dale Earnhardt stuff but I bought a lot more. I do have plans to build a house. You wouldn't believe – when Earnhardt got off the helicopter, he had an old pair of black work shoes on and an old pair of blue jeans, but had a nice shirt on. I said, "Look at him. That's Dale Earnhardt. It's just like I've known him all of my life. He's just like one of the guys around here where I live."

The money was nice, but just spending time with Earnhardt was worth more.

Courtesy of IMHF

Dale and Son Dale Jr.

His Job Is Like Playin' Hooky From Life

Ken Martin

Ken Martin was a NASCAR fan like millions of other people twenty years ago . . . Until he wrote a letter to ESPN that changed his life. Martin was the man behind arguably the most famous speech in NASCAR history: Dale's Earnhardt's speech at the 1994 NASCAR banquet . . . A speech that was replayed many times after Dale's passing. Martin is with the Lingner Group, a highly-respected video production company.

I feel real fortunate that I was able to spend some time with Dale and get to know him pretty well. Growing up as a race fan, the opportunity to work with a lot of these guys is a real neat experience. I did get to spend some time with Dale right after he won his seventh championship in 1994. That was pretty neat.

The way it started out, when Dale won his seventh championship, he clinched it at Rockingham. We had been producing the NASCAR/Winston Cup awards banquet so right after that we were deciding what we could do for this seventh championship that would be different and interesting and compelling and things like that. Working with the folks from R. J. Reynolds, we were like, "Let's have Dale do his own tribute. Let him sort of write and produce it." We told Dale the idea, the people from Winston and Terry Lingner convinced Dale. Dale said the only way he could do it was if we let somebody work with him – some historian or somebody who "knows my background who can remind me of things and stir my memory and remind me of who I should thank and things like that." Terry was like, "We've got the guy for you. We've got the guy who can do that." That guy was me.

The idea to do the speech at the 1994 NASCAR banquet was probably Terry Lingner's, who owns our company and who has always been an inspiration to all of us. After Dale had won the championship, we talked about what could we do, how could we do it. I'm not really sure if it was his idea or my idea, it was something we just kicked around. He told the people from Winston about our idea and they thought it was a good idea and wanted to talk to Dale about it, and I wasn't in on the initial call. After they talked to Dale, he said he needed a historian who could go with him and remind him of things and travel with him for a couple of days. I think Terry knew that was right up my alley. That was perfect for me. I'd certainly give credit to Terry for that idea. He sold Dale on the idea, and it was sort of up to me to execute it – to pull it off.

I've known Terry Lingner for twenty years. I was the ESPN NASCAR historian for all of the early years of its coverage. But the thing he would always come to me for was, "What would the fans want to see here? What do they really care about?" I fortunately had a real heartbeat for what fans want to see and what fans like and helped shape and mold the way we present things. I'm amazed sometimes. I'm like, 'Hey, they like the same things that I do. They enjoy the same stories that I do. They like to remember the same people that I do."

I had interviewed Dale a few times in the past and I had worked with him on a couple of things. Honestly, I wasn't an Earnhardt fan. I always felt like he was aloof, arrogant, and hard to get along with. I respected him a great deal but I felt this wasn't going to be an easy task, but I would tackle it the way I think will serve everybody well. Dale said he had a busy couple of days testing in Talladega, had to go to QVC, other things to do, but just wanted somebody to hang around with him for a couple of days to help him write this stuff.

I was to fly down from Indianapolis to Atlanta on Halloween day in a commercial jet. Dale was going to come through Atlanta and pick me up at the airport on his jet and I would fly with him over to Talladega while he tested and did the other things he needed to do. I fly to Atlanta the next morning. I'm waiting, and Dale comes pulling up in his Lear jet. They throw open the door. I go out and get on board. That was where it all began. I told Dale right off the bat that what we had to do was going to be really interesting, really compelling. But I said, "Dale, I've got to tell you right from the start I'm not a fan of yours. I'm a fan of an obscure driver from Virginia named Lennie Pond, who isn't even racing any more." He was the 1973 NASCAR/Winston Cup Rookie of the Year. He beat Darrell Waltrip for the title. I'm from Virginia, and I was always a fan of his. I told Dale I remembered him coming to South Boston Speedway in the early '70's driving a pickup truck pulling an old beat-up number eight behind it. I said, "I know where you came from, and I know how much success you've had." He liked the fact that I wasn't a worshiper of his. I told him about going to South Boston Speedway and Southside Speedway in the seventies as a teenager and watching him race. He knew that I wasn't a Johnnie-come-lately as far as information. He knew that I knew him from way back.

On the jet, it's just Dale and me, and Tony Eury, Sr., who is the crew chief for Dale Earnhardt, Jr. We start talking and I tell him a little bit about my background and what my goals for this project were. I tell him the key to the project is pictures to match the words. For TV the words are important, but the pictures are even more important. As we were getting ready to land at the airstrip at Talladega, Dale's pilot told him that Richard Childress' plane was approaching from the other direction. Dale was like, "We've got to beat Childress to the ground. If we don't beat Childress to the ground, you're fired." We swoop down over the track at Talladega and hit the landing strip. I felt like we were running three hundred miles an hour when we hit the ground at the landing strip, the pilot put the brakes on for all it was worth. We beat Childress' plane to the terminal. Immediately Dale was at the door, throwing open the door, jumping out on the ground, saying, "We beat you guys." The pilot came back to me and apologized and said, "Believe me, that is not a standard FAA-approved landing." But it was just Dale's competitive side – wanting to win in everything.

When we go in at Talladega, Richard Childress and others come down. The car isn't ready to test so we sit down and talk about who we want to thank, how we want to do things. We talk some and visit some, but he's busy testing. Originally I'm planning to stay at the Holiday Inn with the team. At the end of the day, Dale said, "We just haven't got nearly as much done as I had hoped. I'm staying at a friend's condo here over on the lake, why don't you just come stay with me. We can have more private time and can sit and talk." I just sort of went along. I felt we had sort of begun to bond or whatever. I didn't want to ask for anything. I wanted him to lead the way on this thing.

We go over to the condo. He asked if I wanted to get something to eat. And he had to stop by and see a couple of friends. We went into a couple of restaurants and he talked to a guy named Johnny Ray who owned one of Dale's earliest Winston Cup cars that he had run down at Atlanta. We visited with him for a few minutes there. We stop at a drive-thru of Kentucky Fried Chicken and get chicken. Then we go back to the condo. We sit and eat and talk. I've got a tape recorder so I wanted to start getting down some of these things – people and facts and all on tape to help me remember. For the next three or four hours, we sit and talk about these things. I do some recording and some writing and formulating things through my mind. We get up the next morning, and head back to the track, stop at a convenience store, buy a box of Cheerios and a couple of Styrofoam cups, and we stand out in the parking lot eating Cheerios out of a Styrofoam cup. We were driving through the countryside at Talladega and he wanted to show me a couple of horse farms and things down there of folks he knew. I thought it was a really neat, unique experience. I thought it was wonderful. All this time, we just continue to talk. He tests again at the track that day. It happens that on that day, it was the first time that he's going to let Dale, Jr. go out in Dale, Sr.'s car and test. At this time, seven years ago, so Dale, Jr. is only seventeen or eighteen years old. Dale, Sr. tells me not to tell anybody about this. He didn't want a big deal made out of it. He just wanted to let Dale, Jr. get out on the track and get a little track time and get a little feel for it. "Don't make any big deal about it," Dale, Sr. said.

Dale and I were up on top of the truck while they were working on the car. They had one garage all to themselves. There was another garage at Talladega that a couple of other Chevy teams were testing at, but it was basically just Dale's Busch team and Richard Childress' Winston Cup team there. We were up on the hauler. Dale, Jr. had been walking around the garage area, sort of moping around like a teenager. I'll never forget, Dale, Jr. was walking around and looked up at the hauler. Dale, Sr. had his uniform on, and he just looked at him and gave the front of his uniform a tug, just to give Dale Jr. the sign to go put his uniform on. Immediately Junior turns around, hops up and heads into the trailer, and three minutes later, he's out wearing this Sun Drop Soda uniform and looking like a kid who's getting ready to start the challenge of a lifetime. Dale, Sr. is up there looking at him like, "I remember what that was like."

I felt their relationship was typical father-son. I told Dale I had a teenage son, and I know what that's like as a dad. It was a loving relationship but like at Talladega while I went and stayed with Dale, Sr. at the condo, he sent Dale, Jr. to sleep with the team at the Holiday Inn. He wanted him to stay with the Busch team guys so he would build a relationship with those guys, to feel like he was part of that team. Dale felt like if Dale, Jr. had come and stayed at the condo, he wouldn't have been able to talk as much.

When Dale Jr. goes out on the track, Dale, Sr. immediately gets his stopwatch out. Honestly, within three or four laps, he was as fast as Dale, Sr. was. I thought it was really amazing, but Dale, Sr. said, "Nah, anybody can drive that fast." But you could tell he was proud and happy that his son had gone out and run well that first time out.

At the end of the day, Dale told me he had to go do a QVC appearance in King of Prussia, Pennsylvania. He had just won his seventh championship the week before so they knew it would be a big night for QVC. He asked me to go with him so we could still talk. He had a Lear jet, the fastest available, which had the required two pilots, and was an incredibly fast airplane. His thing was, "I'm in a Hurry and Don't Know Why," a song by Alabama. Dale and I were along, with the pilots, and he felt we could get a lot done between Talladega and Charlotte where he had to stop and pick up Don Hawk, his business manager, who was going with us up to QVC.

After we picked up Don, Dale asked him what the record for QVC, the most money sold by an athlete in an hour, and two hours. Don was spouting out figures for Shaquille O'Neal, and Rusty Wallace. Dale said, "We were going to blow that away. We're going to double those numbers."

We land at a small private landing strip and a limo is there waiting. Amazingly when we land, there are dozens and dozens of people on the ground at the airport waiting there for Dale to get autographs and things like that. They knew he was coming to be on QVC so knew to expect a plane in and they were there. He stopped and signed autographs, and then we went and got in the car. It was about 8:30 at night and was cool and rainy. We drove about fifteen or twenty miles to the QVC headquarters. When we get ready to turn into the driveway, the road is practically blocked with fans waiting for Dale, hoping for autographs and things like that. We stop, he signs some autographs. Then we go park and go into the building. Everybody there is yelling and cheering – seven time champion! His business manager and I sit in the green room while Dale goes out on the air. In the green room, there is a computer, which shows a tally of how much is being sold. Dale can look through the glass at us in there and Don kept giving him the thumbs-up sign

Finally, in like thirty-five minutes, he broke the all-time hour record that they had sold on QVC. Don gave him the big sign, "You're still the champ. You're number one. You just broke the QVC record." He was really happy about that.

After the show is over, I tell him I have to get back to Indianapolis and start writing this thing because we were really under a tight time constraint of less than two weeks to get this whole thing pulled together. I had to get to Philadelphia to catch a flight. I told him I would have a rough draft of the script and material and fax it to him. The limo drops Dale off at King of Prussia. He gives the limo driver a hundred dollar bill and says, "Take care of this guy. Get him to the Philadelphia airport safely." It was about one in the morning. I felt it was so surreal – here was Dale taking care of me and wanting to make sure I get home safely.

I get to Indianapolis and start writing the first draft of what turned out to be the 'thank you video.' I write it and fax it down to Dale. We talk on the phone about some of the people and how we are going to do things. He's really happy with what I have written. I told him that in a couple of days when he went to Atlanta for the race, I would be there. I wanted him and Teresa to take the script and pull out all the photos and things you have to match with these words. I stressed that this was TV so we had to have picture to go along with these words.

On that Friday after qualifying, I meet Dale and Teresa in their motor home. We all sit there for a couple of hours, and they pull out these old photos.

When I showed Dale Earnhardt the preview of the video, I was a little bit nervous but I knew that it was good. I knew it would exceed Dale's expectations because when he left here after doing the voiceover and all, he was down a little. He felt he wasn't as good as he hoped to be. I told him not to worry about it. We could edit the stuff and pull this stuff up. I said, "Believe me, you'll be amazed at how good it can turn out." I knew that it was good, and everybody who had seen it before Dale – everybody here at the office said, "Man, this is unbelievable how good this thing turned out."

We were in a suite at the Waldorf looking at it. I was sitting down, and he and Teresa were standing a couple of feet away. I was just sort of watching him and Teresa was the first one to get a few tears in her eyes, and then I saw Dale. I was sitting there, and when it finished, Dale started walking towards me. He grabbed me by my hand to shake my hand and pulled me up out of the chair and hugged me. It was pretty cool.

All this happened so quickly that a lot of my friends didn't really know what I was doing. It was like on a Monday that it was decided I would do it, and on Tuesday I was heading for Atlanta. Part of the thing that made it so great was that it was so personal that I got to spend three days alone with Dale, just me and him talking. We're sitting in a condo in Talladega eating friend chicken. I'm sitting at a drive-thru window with Dale Earnhardt.

We pulled up to a convenience store. Dale said he really wanted a beer. He wanted me to go into the store to get it. I went, "Dale, I'm a Christian. I don't drink. I don't buy beer. If you want a beer, you're going to have to go get it." He walked right into that convenience store, came out to the car with two Coors Lights, handed me the keys to the car. He said, "You drive. I cannot get stopped with alcohol on my breath. You drive." He said for me to drive and he would tell me where to go. We drove around some through the Alabama countryside. It was one of the things that Dale really respected about me. Even though I was here with the great Dale Earnhardt, I still wasn't going to change my values. I think Dale really respected that. I think almost right off the bat, he was gonna see if I was going to back off on my beliefs even though a lot of things I had expressed to him. I think he kinda got a kick out of it.

I think he grew in his Christian faith over the years and was in pretty good shape with the Lord when he died. I know that people from MRO (Motor Racing Outreach) really felt at peace that Dale was exactly where he needed to it in his walk with Christ. I do, too. In my Sunday school class at church here, after the death, a lot of people there knew I had this relationship with Dale. They were all asking, "Was he a Christian? How do you know?" I said I know because we talked about it. I just knew how much he respected the Christian faith. He talked about how it was almost impossible for him to go to church because when he goes to church he's Dale Earnhardt. Traveling with him those days was almost like traveling with a rock star, as far as the adulation. Everywhere he went, people's heads would turn. Everywhere he went people would want a piece of him. On a personal level, I said, "Dale, don't you wish sometimes you could just go shopping with Teresa or go to the movies or go somewhere that you didn't have to be so much in the public eye?" He was like, "Yeah, but the flip side of it isn't bad either." I know that he yearned for some private times and an opportunity to be not held hostage by his popularity.

I'm from Lynchburg, Virginia but have lived in Indianapolis for twelve years. The day of the banquet I called Jeff Motley, a local newspaper writer for the Lynchburg News and Daily Advance, and now he's the PR Director at the Las Vegas Motor Speedway. I thought I had to tell somebody this story because it is so unbelievable about what has happened. Jeff did write a really nice story for the Lynchburg newspaper. It was printed in the afternoon paper because I had told him highlights of what had happened so he could write the article. Any time I tell people the story, it is so unbelievable that I've been so blessed in my life. I could tell you a hundred stories that would just make your hair stand on end as far as things that have happened in my career, as far as working with people who had been my heroes and been able to produce thirteen documentaries in the last three years and write about these guys. Just to sit in Richard Petty's log cabin and talk to him for a couple of hours. And to sit with Fred Lorenzen from Elmhurst, Illinois who, when I was a kid growing up, was the 'Golden Boy.' He was my childhood idol, and to get to go to his house and do a couple of hours interview with him. I've lived a blessed, charmed life. I'm still a fan.

I have a picture that Dale Earnhardt personalized and autographed to me. He gave me a pocketknife that's really a prized possession. It was a special knife he'd had made when he won his seventh championship. After he saw the video, he brought it to me to the banquet in New York.

He said, "This is a knife I had made for some special friends as a com-memoration of my championship." It's a little lock-blade pocketknife that's got 'Dale Earnhardt, Seven Time NASCAR/Winston Cup Champion.' He gave it to me. I always kept it in a special place. Now, I have it being framed, along with the picture he gave me, personalized and signed.

From the very start with him, I didn't ask for autographs. I didn't ask for pictures. I didn't want to ask for any of those things just because I saw how he was constantly being asked for them. I just sort of said, "I'm not going to ask him for those things." This picture he gave me was one of his championship photos. When we were on the plane from Charlotte to QVC, he had one of the pictures and said, "Can I give you one of these?" He said, "Okay, what's your wife's name?" He wrote, 'To Becky and Ken. Thanks. Dale Earnhardt.' I didn't want to ask him for things. I just wanted to try to keep our relationship such that we were friends. I didn't want to try to become a fan to him. I regret that now, but at the time I just felt like it was the right way to handle it, the right way to treat him. I'm sorry I don't have pictures and mementoes and things like that, but that's just the way things are.

For the first thirty years of my life, all I was was a fan of NASCAR. When I was born my dad was the promoter of a short track in Lynchburg at Schrader Field. He also was a Wynn's Friction Proofing distributor, an oil additive. I grew up going to races with my mom and dad. I went to Daytona in 1958 for the last Beach race, on the beach. I drove by the Daytona Speedway when I was six years old, and it was under construction. I went to my first Southern 500 in 1961. I just grew up a fan of the sport, but as a fan of the sport, I collected programs, memorabilia, news articles, news clippings, and I would go every Friday/Saturday night to the local short tracks around Virginia Southside Speedway in Richmond, South Boston Speedway in Virginia. I just grew up as a fan of the sport.

In 1981, I owned a hardware store and was an insurance agent for Nationwide Insurance. I was thirty years old and was not really happy with my career. I was working hard but not really happy with how things were going. ESPN had just started doing NASCAR races. We didn't have cable TV in our home so I went to my mom and dad's house to watch a race they were doing. I sat there and watched; this was only the sixth or seventh race that ESPN had ever done. I watched it and said, "These guys don't know anything about NASCAR. They just don't know." The next day, I called ESPN headquarters in Bristol, Connecticut and said, "Who is in charge of your NASCAR races?" They said Terry Lingner is the guy in charge of the NASCAR broadcasts. I sat down and wrote Terry about a three-page letter telling him what was wrong with the way they were covering the NASCAR races. I wrote here's what the fans want to see, here's a better way to cover it, here's the way to do it. I mailed it and about five days later at my hardware store, the phone rings. Our secretary tells me that a Terry Lingner was on the phone for me. I think here's some big-time network TV guy who's going to chew me out. Terry says, "I read your letter. You're right. We really don't know anything about NASCAR, and it sounds like you do. We're going to be doing a race over in Richmond, Virginia in just a week or so. Do you want to come over, and I'd love to meet you." I'm like, "Sure, what do you want me to do?" He said he would tell me when I got there.

So I drove over to Richmond. I had never worked TV or anything like that in my life. He introduced me to Bob Jenkins and Larry Nuber, who were the play-by-play and color guys. Terry said, "I want you to go up into the booth with Larry and Bob. I want you to write them notes about how to do things better, about what to say about some of these guys, about some of the background, what are we watching, how can we help things out?" I'm like, "Okay." I thought this can't be happening. I went to the store and bought a stack of index cards. As soon as the race started, I just started writing notes and handing them to Bob and Larry about different drivers, different backgrounds, here's these guys' records, just things I knew off the top of my head. About two thirds of the way through the race, I gave Larry Nuber a note which said, "Bobby Allison is going to win this race. I've been tracking their pit stop strategy. Bobby is going to make it on one less pit stop." Larry looks at me like, "What?" I showed him a chart showing here's where Bobby pitted, here's where Tim Richmond pitted, here's where the others guys pitted. So then Larry is on the air saying, "We've calculated that Bobby Allison will have one less pit stop, and Bobby wins the race." After the race is over, which Allison won, we go down to the truck. Bob and Larry say, "You've got to hire this guy." This is all really like a dream, but I'm so naïve I really don't know any different. It does feel like I'm dreaming.

I had brought with me a bunch of old photos from Lynchburg Speedway from the early fifties and pictures of me down at the starting line at the Beach race in 1958. I'm showing all these things to Terry. I'm two years old at the Martinsville Speedway standing behind an old modified car. Everybody in the office loves to see this picture of me standing at the track. It was sort of like it was meant to be.

Terry said, "I have no money for you. I have no budget. I don't even know what to call this position. If you want to continue to do these things, I'd love to have you, and we'll figure something out." I had these other careers and things going so for a couple of years, I would just travel on the weekends. I would drive. I would share rooms with other guys on the crew. Terry, in the meantime, progressed at ESPN to be a vice president, and he left as the race-to-race producer. He was the coordinating producer. We kept in touch. Terry always said, "Some day, I'm going to make it worth your while." I told him I'm loving what I'm doing. I'm traveling to the races. I went to about one hundred and fifty races in a six or eight year period. Then in late 1988, Terry decided to leave ESPN proper and to form Lingner Group. He called me and said he was moving to Indianapolis and asked if Becky and I would be interested in going there. He was going to start this company. I ask, "What do you want me to do?" He told me to write him a job description. I wrote a job description of what I thought I could do and what I could contribute to the company and faxed it to him. He called me up and said, "Perfect. That's exactly what I want you to do."

In June of 1989, my wife and three children and I moved from Lynchburg Virginia, our lifelong home. I was thirty-seven years old. It wasn't like I was I was some spring chicken. We picked up and moved to Indianapolis. It's been an incredible twelve years when I've had the opportunity to write and produce documentaries for a racing series that we've been involved with, and had the chance to meet everyone of my childhood heroes.

In 1992 when Alan Kulwicki won the championship, I had the opportunity to produce his banquet video. Alan was always known as a real stoic guy who had no emotion. My goal was to make Alan Kulwicki cry. That's my goal. I want people to see another side of Alan Kulwicki. I called his step-mom and I drove up to Milwaukee and talked to Alan's dad and step-mom about Alan. I found out about a brother he had named Kenny who had died of a blood disorder during Alan's teen years. I always noticed that Alan, on his uniform, had this little 'mighty mouse symbol' that he would wear on his uniform. His dad said, "You know, that's his brother, Kenny. That is sort of a driving force in Alan's life." I had never known about Kenny, and people had never known about Kenny until his dad told me about him. Alan had left word that for his championship video, he wanted it to be "My Way," the Frank Sinatra song – that's what he wanted. So with the help of Alan's step-mom and dad, I got a lot of photos of Alan as a kid, and of Alan with his brother Kenny. We put it together into this video that was played at Alan's tribute at the '92 Winston Cup banquet. So we played it for him, without him knowing that this was what the tribute was going to be. He watches it and he sees pictures of him and his little brother riding in his little toy car and things like that. There are tears in his eyes. It was another huge emotional moment. Then tragically less than five months later, Alan is killed in a plane crash. The priest who is to perform Alan's funeral calls me and says, "That 'My Way' video that you did for him meant so much to him, we want to play that as his eulogy at the funeral." I'm like, "How can this be?" – some guy from Lynchburg, Virginia – the old hardware guy – puts together the video that is the eulogy to be played at Alan Kulwicki's funeral?"

Also, I know that God put me in this position for a reason and I never doubt that for a moment. Also, I know that God prepared me for some reason all of those years when I never had any dream that I'd ever work in TV. I'm a history major from Lynchburg College. My goal was to teach history; I loved history. I had zero background in broadcasting. Terry's thing was, "You're a fan. You know the history. You know the sport, and I'll teach you the TV side of it." That's the way that it worked. I knew the sport. I knew the history. I still had a heartbeat for the fan. He taught me how to do TV. But he taught me to do it in such a way that I'm not afraid to show the emotion. I'm not afraid to pull out the best in people. That's what I've always tried to do.

Think how different my life would have been if I'd never written that letter. I think about it a lot. My wife will verify all this. Sometimes I'll just walk up to her, just sort of stunned, like, "How did we get here? How did we get to this place?" We know. We ask the question rhetorically. We know that it was God opening the doors for us. We know that it was His leadership. We just know that.

If I hadn't met that success with Kulwicki, I may have been more intimidated to do Earnhardt. Because I was able to accomplish my goals with Alan, I felt sure that I could do it with Dale. I think everything we do in our life is a building block. Everything that's happened to me in the previous forty-nine years has prepared me for today. Sometimes things happen that were like "Why is this happening to me today?" But six months down the road, it's like – "Oh, that's why it happened. This is what that was all about." The days that I was just a fan, but I still collected those programs, and I still put those things away, I'm like – that's why I did it. That's why those things are still in the file cabinet here. I never take it for granted.

I've been a Christian almost all my life. I accepted Christ when I was twelve years old. I grew up in a Christian home – my mom and dad, sister, wife. I grew up in Christian circles. My great grandfather was a Pentecostal holiness preacher. But I really feel like that NASCAR fans look at their drivers as heroes because they do have to lead a clean lifestyle. They can't abuse their bodies, and also they know that your life can end in a millisecond, just like it did to Dale Earnhardt. I think because of that they do put more trust and faith than some others. I think that's one of the things that's so intriguing about the sport. On the other hand, it's an alcohol and tobacco sport – it's a sport sponsored by alcohol and tobacco. A lot of things that I don't care about, that I don't consume or use, and are not used in my family. But I still think fans can look at it and separate that from the sport.

Terry Lingner has done more to influence the way Americans look at stock car racing – more than any other person. He literally wrote the book on how television would cover stock car racing. I was happy to contribute to that. Terry has always been wanting to give more credit to the other people who work around him, but without his leadership, without his motivation, without his ability to put the right people in the right place, and then let them do their thing, none of us would be as successful as we are. For the last twenty years, Terry has basically shaped the way that America looks at motor sports. He's been recognized as one of the most influential people by Stock Car Racing magazine and other things. But still, his name is one that most of the racing public does not recognize. Our company doesn't have PR people. Our company doesn't have press agents. We don't put out press releases talking about how great we are or what we do. We do it because we're fans. We do it because we want to do it, not because we want adoration or adulation or anything else.

Two days after Dale passed, we aired a show called "A Tribute to Dale Earnhardt" on ESPN. I started writing the show deciding which video pieces to use. Terry was like, "How can we close this show?" I said the only way to close it is with Dale's tribute. When Dale had the forum after winning seven championships, anything he wanted to say and do he could have done. What did he do? He chose to thank all the people who helped him to that point in his career. I said, "Why not play it again. That's like him writing his own eulogy." We pulled out the piece from six years earlier and sat and looked at it, and thought, "Man, it's perfect. It's perfect." It was emotional. We thought about what went into making it the first time. Really, I think it did play perfectly. It was amazing how little had changed since the time he won he seventh championship as far as people who were influential in his life and people who meant a lot to him. It just seemed to be the right thing and the right feeling. Everybody who has given us feedback about the show just talked about how meaningful it was to hear Dale say those things.

It was a privilege to get to know Dale Earnhardt personally. It was gratifying for me to know that this driver, who was recognized and adored by millions of fans, that I got to know that he was worthy of that adoration, that he was worthy of the fans' praise. He was talented as a driver. He was a loving father and husband. He truly was an icon of the sport for the twentieth century. A hundred years from now, when drivers are measured, they will be measured against the ruler that Dale Earnhardt established.

"Dad, Is Sam The Best Painter Of Cars Ever?" "No, Son, Earl Scheib Is."

Sam Bass

Sam Bass has gained renown for his paintings of Winston Cup racers and also for the colorful, artful designs on many of the race cars. Bass became Dale Earnhardt's artist for many of his cars. Bass artfully recalls their relationship.

In late sixties and early seventies, I started going to races with my uncles. They took me to the race tracks – originally Southside Speedway in Richmond Virginia. Then we started going to the close tracks – Richmond and Martinsville, Virginia and Rockingham and Darlington. I just loved the sport – everything about it, the speed, the color, the excitement. I'd always, as a child, been interested in drawing and painting. It just made sense that the things I drew and painted were race cars. When I was six or seven years old, I was already doing drawings and paintings of race cars and of my heroes, Bobby Allison, David Pearson and Richard Petty, et cetera.

I had been producing art work from the early '80's and in '87, I went into business full time. I really got a big break at Talladega in 1981 when I took one of my pieces of art work to the garage area to have Bobby Allison sign it. While I was in the garage area, several team representatives asked me about doing paintings for them and their drivers. In the early eighties, everything kind of snowballed. It got to the point where I couldn't keep up with everything that was going on on a part time basis. I decided to go full time with it in August of 1987.

I met Dale about 1984. I had done a piece of art work for myself of Dale in the Wrangler car. In Richmond Virginia, I showed it to some of the people there and they were very interested in buying my painting for the unheard of price of three hundred dollars for the original painting. I was excited about that. They wanted to do it right then and there. It would really mean a lot to me, but I wanted to make sure that Dale liked it. So I took the painting to him to get his approval and asked him if it would be okay if I sold it, and also to ask him what his royalty rate would be – what I would owe him out of the transaction. He looked at me, with his grin, and said, "No, that's okay, they're my sponsor, go ahead." And so I did. Well, lo and behold, that kind of began our working relationship. I don't know what it was but I think he liked the art work and I guess trusted me.

The thing that has been so amazing to me since this tragedy happened are the stories I have heard from his friends and relatives about how much he thought of my art work and how much he trusted me. That has just been so amazing because Dale is a man of few words. He made every word he said be very important, but he never said a lot. The stories and everything that people share with me about what he thought of what I did for him, and how much he cared about me and my art work has just meant the world to me. I always knew it but he wasn't the type of person who would really spend a lot of time telling you that. So it was a pretty neat thing.

After I sold the first painting, I ended up doing a real neat piece of art work for a transporter design for Richard Childress that featured Dale Earnhardt and the Monte Carlo. This was a couple of years later. I got to work with all of them. It was really a kind of neat trendsetter from the standpoint that it had this huge portrait of Dale and the car on the side of the transporter. I did the original art, and they projected it up and painted it and everything. But that was really neat. I got to work with them then, and I've done just about every transporter design for Childress since that point.

Actually the way it all happened. Wrangler contacted me, from the original sale of that first painting, and we started doing some work together. They wanted me to do a bumper sticker for them. I did this bumper sticker design and because of the horizontal format of it, I kinda said, "Hey, you might want to think about this thing as a transporter layout. It was just one of those lucky things where they hadn't come up with anything yet at that point, and it lended itself very well to the transporter, so it was pretty cool. They liked it, and it was a very successful thing. Knowing how conscientious he was about the way things were portrayed and how things were presented, I have no doubt in my mind that if he didn't like it, the thing would have been repainted. So I always consider myself very fortunate. I tell everybody that you can define the word 'intimidation' any way you want to, but for me it was always doing a piece of art work and taking it to Dale and just making sure he liked it. That few minutes there when you're standing there and he's looking it over, or whatever, you just can feel your heart pounding in your chest and you want to make sure that he was happy with what you did. Fortunately for me, I never had too many situations when he wasn't happy with what I did.

There's been a number of things – meeting Richard Childress, working with Dale from the mid-eighties, and they were kind enough to introduce me to the Goodwrench people, et cetera. I had some input. One of the really special things I got a chance to do was do the paint scheme for the Wheaties car that Dale ran in the Winston. That was just a chance in a lifetime honor, because obviously it's real important for an athlete to be on a box of Wheaties. Lord knows I'll never be on a box of Wheaties personally. It was just such a neat thing. I designed the car and then Wheaties decided they wanted to put Dale on the Wheaties box. Dale told them he would really like for me to design the box. I had designed the car, but he wanted me to design the box. I did a piece of artwork, whereas I usually use photography, and they used it on the box, and of course he ran the Wheaties car. I got to unveil the painting with Dale down in Atlanta when they announced this whole promotion. It had Dale inside the car, kind of a tight driver's head shot with the helmet and goggles and had the whole mike radio setup and everything and in the foreground kind of had the Wheaties car coming at you diagonally in front of him. That was an honor. I knew Dale was proud of that whole thing, and he was the first race driver ever depicted on a box of Wheaties. This debate has raged on forever about 'are drivers really athletes?' To me, if you're on a box of Wheaties, and you're not an athlete, what are you?

So that was kind of a neat thing to get that opportunity. But really, right now, all of the Dale Earnhardt, Inc. cars are my design. He and Teresa have, over the years, given me a chance to design their cars and create that team look for Pennzoil, Budweiser and NAPA. I've done a lot of special paint schemes with him over the years, as recent as this year, the paint scheme he ran in the Bud Shootout, the Oreo car, was my design. Then there have been really, really neat things. He had me design their Lear jet and the art work for their Newell coach, or their corporate logos and letterhead in various companies they've opened up. I got asked to do that even as far back as being asked to design the paint schemes when his children, Dale, Jr., Kelly and Kerry ran their late-model stock cars. They had me do that stuff. He kept me very, very busy, and he always kept me on my toes. It was nothing for him to show up at the back door of my office early one morning and say, "Hey, I'm getting ready to go over and watch the Busch practice and we're going to be back in about an hour and a half. I need this and that." It was always challenging, but it was always fun. I always knew he appreciated it. One of the rush items was the Newell Coach design that I mentioned. The thing was in the paint booth in the Newell Coach plant out West. They had faxed him a design that they were going to put on it, and he wasn't real sure that was exactly what he wanted so he came by and brought me the line art and everything else of the Coach design and said, "Hey, can you work on this for me?" He came back in about two hours, and I had about five different designs laid out. He kind of wanted to tweak all of the designs to come up with exactly what he wanted. By five thirty that night, I was out at the farm, and he and Teresa had picked what they wanted, and I was on my way to Federal Express to get it out to them.

He gave me one of the biggest compliments that day I've ever received. He said, "You know, it's incredible that you can walk into a man's office early in the morning unexpected, and by that afternoon, he's done taken care of you." That's what this business for me has always been about – just trying to do great work for people and have that relationship because that's what it's all about.

One of the funny things about Dale is that he knew what he wanted, and he would challenge you to give it to him. You knew when you had pleased him and come up with what he wanted to see. You knew you had really accomplished something. I never will forget whenever I carried out the designs for the kids' cars for the late-model stock cars, on the initial pass I carried out there to him, I had the numbers leaning to the right. In other words they were leaning back to the rear wheels of the car. If you know anything about Dale's numbers on his number three car, they lean to the front. He said, "Let me ask you something. Why do you have these numbers leaning back like this?" I said, "Well, you know, there's two schools of thought. There is one that says if you lean them forward, they're moving forward with the car. But if you lean them back, it looks like the wind's blowing them back 'cause the car's moving so fast." He looked at me and said, "Well in my opinion there's only one school of thought." He stood up, and he said, "When you run, do you run like this, and he leaned forward. Or do you run like this, and he leaned backward." From that point, I knew not to ever take him any number styles that didn't lean forward. But to see Dale Earnhardt doing that, that was just a really, really neat special moment. There were so many things I can look back on now and realize the time you got to spend with him was just so very special.

Sweet Home Alabama

Betty Carlan

If you visit the International Motorsports Hall of Fame, a beautiful facility located at the entrance to the awe-inspiring Talladega race track in Talladega, Alabama, you will see dozens of colorful race cars displayed from racing's past. In the memorabilia lined library of the museum is a friendly, zealous keeper of the flame sitting behind her desk. Betty Carlan knows as much about the history of motorsports as most degreed professors, and she has more friends in the sport than almost anyone else. Mrs. Carlan – her hometown Alabama friends pronounce her first name with an 'i' as in 'Bitty,' has been a close friend of the entire Earnhardt family over the past decade.

In the early 1970's, I ran a drivers-ed program for the handicapped when I was with the state Department of Education, and they told me I needed to do something spectacular, or I was going to lose my funding. And the most spectacular thing around was the Talladega Superspeedway. I brought five hundred special-ed kids up to the Speedway and they had the run of the track. Bobby Allison talked to them and showed them his car, and I was hooked on racing.

We did it again with Raymond Williams, who was Captain America, and then Richard Childress came one year, and Richard Petty. I always had gobs of kids, and radio and newspaper coverage, and I started going to all the races. I became Don Naman's outside contact person and scored a couple of races and got hooked on that, and my devotion to the sport just grew and grew and grew.

I moved back to North Carolina in '77 and lived there until '92. I was working in education, and at the same time scored for Cale Yarborough, and I rented a house from Richard Petty, and started scoring for him.

I came back to Talladega in '92, and that's when I officially got to know Dale. I began work as the librarian for the International Motorsport Hall of Fame here in Talladega.

And way back then, when I was working for the state department, I was making more money than the drivers, and they were always hungry, so I'd carry a great big cooler in the trunk of my car, and I made sandwiches for everybody out there. So when I moved back to Talladega, they said, "Okay, are you still going to feed us?" And I said, "Yes," except now I bring crock pots and feed them warm food. More than likely I will fix them country fried steak, creamed potatoes, some sort of vegetable, a salad and dessert. You have to plan ahead.

The entire Richard Childress team came down here to test, and Childress called me and said, "We're going to be down to you. What day do you want to feed us?" So I chose the day, and everybody who worked for Childress came. There must have been twenty-five people in here, and that's when I really got to know Dale. I became a Dale Earnhardt fan that minute, because he was one of the nicest people I ever met in my life.

When they arrived, Richard grabbed me and hugged me, and then Dale grabbed me and hugged me, and I said, "Richard, I do not know your driver." Dale said, "Oh Betty, but I know you." And I thought, "Oh God, he must be thinking, Who is that crazy ole woman?" But he was just a friendly, friendly, nice person. He knew more about me than I knew about him. It was just instant friendship, and he teased me unmercifully every time I saw him about everything under the sun that he could think to tease me about.

I always cover the window of the library and lock the door so people can't walk by and gaze through the window while we're sitting here eating. That first day, Dale leaned back, and he said, "I sure would like to see the museum."

I said, "So, go look."
He said, "You got the door locked."
I said, "Aren't you mechanically inclined enough to turn that little knob?"
"Well, yes, but you'll lock it behind me and won't let me back in."
I said, "Oh, go look at the museum. I'll let you back in." But it was that sort of picking, yackety yackety, back and forth every time I ever saw him.

And through Ralph being inducted into the Hall of Fame, I got to meet Dale's mom, Martha. I had a hard time finding information on Ralph, because he died so long ago, so I called everybody I thought had ever seen Ralph Earnhardt race or knew anything about him, and I got Martha's phone number, and I'd call and verify with her, and I asked her once when I was talking to her if she was coming to the induction. She said, "I don't know anybody down there."

I said, "Yes, you do. You know me."

She said, "Just on the phone."

I said, "Okay, I will just come up and visit my daughter, who lives in North Carolina, and we'll come over, and you can meet me, and then you'll know somebody down here."

So I did, and about two weeks before the induction, Dale called down here, and he said, "Who's going to take care of mama while she's down there?" And they said, "Betty Carlan." And he said, "Good. Then I'll let her come."

So Martha came down for the induction, and I met her plane, and stayed with her in Birmingham and got her on the plane Thursday night to go back home.

Martha and I became instant friends. That whole family is so great, and the minute you meet one of them – instant friends.

It was a very emotional weekend for her, and we just gossiped in general. By this time, we had talked so much on the phone that we were friends, and what do you talk about with your friends?

We even rewrote her speech. She said, "There's a thing or two in here that I don't really like." Somebody else had written it, and she said, "There are things I want to change." We were over in the motel in Birmingham. I said, "All right, let me borrow a laptop, and we'll rewrite it." So we rewrote it the morning before she was going to give it.

Dale was there, too, and both brothers and their wives and both sisters and their husbands. They are all involved working with Dale one way or another. They are great folks, and they tease, too.

I remember one time Jeannie Barnes gave me an artist's proof of her rendition of 'The Man." It is an absolutely fantastic painting! Dale is sitting on the pit wall with the seat propped up on a jack stand, and the car is back behind him.

And I know all these guys too well – I don't ask for autographs, but when Dale came in the museum that time, I said, "Dale, you know I don't ever ask for an autograph."

He said, "Yeah, I know."

I said, "But I do have something I want you to sign for me."

He said, "Well, what is it?" And I told him Jean had given me this artist proof, and he said, "Well, get it out. Where is it?"
I said, "It's locked in the closet."
He said, "Locked in the closet?"
I said, "Yes."
He said, "Get the thing out, and let me sign it for you." And he did. And it's hanging in my home.

I think the last time I saw Dale was when they unveiled his Wrangler car out in the pavilion of the museum. They held a press conference here. It was neat. He was all excited. That was the same car as he won his first championship in. It was the Wrangler car, number 3, blue and yellow. It was on display here at the museum until recently when Richard Childress called all his cars back, out of plain decency, after Dale was killed. And it will be six months before any of them will be released, and we're supposed to get the first one.

After Dale got killed, Richard was afraid people would take pieces of them for souvenirs. See, they stopped selling his cars, because people were reselling them for exorbitant prices. I guess they thought while emotions were still so high, people would tear the decals off. Some of these fans are into getting souvenirs any way they can, and Richard didn't want the cars to get messed up, so he decided to take them back until emotions died down.

We had a memorial service Tuesday night after he died, and we had more than four thousand people here. We didn't start even thinking about it until noontime on Monday, and we got the word out, and got the program organized. My priest, Father Richard Donohoe, came, and he conducted the devotional part. He made me read one of the Bible portions, and then Jim Freeman, the executive director of the Hall of Fame spoke, and Grant Lynch, the general manager of the Talladega Speedway spoke, and then a motivational speaker in town by the name of Brian Townsend spoke, and all of them talked not of the death but of the life of Dale Earnhardt, which is the Catholic way, because Father is Catholic, and I am, too. It was just great, fantastic, and then the next day, we decided to make a Dale Earnhardt Gallery at the museum.

It's full of photos of Dale and his family that are not usually seen. We have artwork from Jean Barnes and Sam Bass, and we've got some coming in by a man named Hill from up in North Carolina, and somebody made a king size quilt that is really, really neat. It has The Intimidator and the date, and it's surrounded by black and white checks.

I called Richard Childress's office on the morning we were going to do it and told his rep I needed a big number 3 that was used on the car.

"Oh, no, we're not letting anybody have those."

I said, "Did you hear what I said? I need a big 3." So they overnighted me one that went on the top of the car, a three-by-four which we have put on a black background. It's neat. You ought to see it.

Richard Childress called me from Bristol. I had left him a message to call me. Dale was going to get the Governor's Award at our Hall of Fame induction on April 19, for the person who has done the most for racing in the area, and Dale Earnhardt IS Talladega. The governor will be here, and we wanted as many of the Earnhardts as felt they could to come, and we wanted Richard and his other drivers to come. Since it was Richard's car, we wanted Richard to come, but he sometimes is a little shy about things – I've known him for thirty years so Jim Freeman asked me to call him and explain what this is, and he hadn't had a chance to call. So he called me from Bristol, and he's coming and whichever of his drivers want to come. Martha said she wasn't able to make it.

The late Neil Bonnett is one of the inductees this year, and we had talked to Dale about being the presenter for Neil, and we think he was going to do it. He was hesitating, only because he was afraid he would break down. He and Neil were best friends, and then we had to find someone else. Bobby Allison is going to do it. Bobby Allison was a mentor for Neil Bonnett. When Bobby was driving the Coke machine, Neil was driving the drink box. Neil was running local tracks, and he was building his cars out of parts Bobby had left over.

When I heard that Dale had been killed, I called Martha as soon as I could get through. I said, "I called you to tell you I loved you, and to ask, 'What in the world can I do for you?'"

She said, "Come to see me." So I dropped everything and went. She is a strong, strong woman but one sweet lady, just absolutely fantastic. I just love her dearly, and if she ever finds out I'd been up to see my daughter and didn't come by to see her, she gets upset. I do my best to come by and see her every time I go up there.

When Dale died, the reaction here in Alabama was just like everywhere else. We all cried a lot. We were very, very upset. We could not believe it. Nobody, I don't think, realized the impact that man had on motorsports, on NASCAR, until he's not there any more. I still look for him. I do, and I probably always will, because he was my driver. I know all the rest of them. Some I like. Some I don't. He hardly ever qualified up front – and so you say, 'There is so-and-so on the pole and so-and -so on the outside front now. Now, let's watch Dale come up through the pack.' And my eyes just automatically went to the right, and I would look for Dale.

A few years ago Dale had a bad crash, and he missed a whole bunch of races, and racing just was not the same, and it isn't now. It just is not. To me, until Dale, Jr. settles down again – bless his heart, if he hadn't had that bad pit stop, he probably would have won that race a month after his dad passed. But I'm crazy about Steve Park, and I'm crazy about Michael Waltrip, and I pull for them real hard, but I want Dale, Jr. to find his place and get back up there and make it exciting again. See, the excitement is gone. It's just so different without Dale out there.

Courtesy of IMHF

Car Owner Richard Childress and Dale Discuss Strategy

Chapter 2

I Love Those Dear Hearts and Gentle People

When We Got All The Way Up To Broke, We Threw A Party

Gray London

Gray London could have been a NASCAR racer. Instead, he went into business and attained success in the vending machine food business. With Ralph Earnhardt's help, he bought a car and began racing in the Charlotte area. At age 13, Dale Earnhardt was his crew chief. When Dale wanted to race, London provided financial assistance. London is writing a book about his experiences called "Driver with a Mission."

I had been into drag racing in Memphis, Tennessee, drove for Chevrolet out there before they were getting into the big-time stuff. I was offered the ride in 1960, either to go into NASCAR or into USAC. I had a little daughter that changed my mind. In 1960, I moved back home to Kannapolis, and started a business there called Dainty Maid Foods. We manufacture products such as sandwiches and all types of vending items, the jellos and salads and all for vending machines for people like Coca Cola, Four C's, Servmation, and Canteen. Then later we made special things for people like Stewarts.

I got back into racing in 1964 when I went to Ralph Earnhardt and asked him to help me get started. He said he didn't have time to build a car, but he would help me find a good car. So I bought my first race car from Ronnie Hopkins down in Greenville, South Carolina. Ralph and my brother went with me, and we went down and loaded it up and bought his truck and everything. Ronnie Hopkins' sons were building the chassis that Dale and others use now. Ronnie was upset with his driver so he was going to get out of racing. Anyway we brought that back to the Earnhardt garage in Kannapolis. We bought everything he had so out of all the parts he had, Ralph and I both ran out of it for two or three years – all the extra engines, his truck and everything.

Naturally that was when I met Dale. He was about twelve years old. He was just a skinny kid, but very intense. He was around the shop there all the time. In fact, part of our things that we were doing was the fact that he was my crew chief. People in Kannapolis or somewhere else or a kid would come up and say, "My dad says you used to race. Were you any good?" I'd say, "I was the best in the world." They'd say, "Oh, you wasn't. I ain't never heard of you." I say, "Well, I was so good. Dale Earnhardt was my crew chief." That sort of gets a laugh. Then I tell them Dale was thirteen, fourteen, fifteen years old.

As crew chief, Dale would beat out all the fenders that he could. He actually would change the 'quick-change rear ends.' He would change the gears from one track to another one. He did all the tire work. His dad would be busy with his own car so Ralph would point out to him things to do, so Dale did a lot of it. Between him and his dad, they kept my car running.

We ran real well, I felt like, to get started. The only two tracks I ran usually were Concord and Metrolina at Charlotte. Occasionally we would go to another town. By that time I was really getting into it and Ralph and Dale maintained two other cars for me. Guys like Larry Wallace and Don Beam and some of those guys drove the other two cars. All the time I drove, my car was kept at the Earnhardt's house. Ralph had a two-stall garage. The one on the right-hand side was mine; the one on the left-hand side was his.

A lot of people claim to have been close to the Earnhardts and to have known them well. Even one guy in a book claimed that, and I don't even know him. Yet I was there for fifteen years. I don't think most of them were really there because I don't hear any of them with the phrases Ralph would use. Some of the things that I was saving for my book, I think they are going to see a little different side, et cetera, of the whole thing. My youngest daughter and I have spent Christmases, Thanksgivings with them. Dale's mother would take my youngest daughter to the races with her. She would go to the races wearing a Harry Gant t-shirt. So we would give Dale a hard time if he didn't win the race. He could drive. If he did win it, he had a big head – just giving him a rough time. She certainly enjoyed it, and she loved Dale's mother, Martha and Brenda, Dale's wife at the time, Junior's mother. We thought the world of her and still do. All the time I have in Dale's life was before Teresa's time. He hadn't made it until then, but we loved Brenda to death and still do. I've lost contact with her. I know she is in Virginia, and I would love to get in touch with her. Maybe somebody will tell me how one day.

Brenda was the daughter of Robert Gee, who at that time was building Darrell Waltrip's '88 Gatorade car, a green and white car. Dale went over one winter I remember and helped build five Lagunas over there for

Waltrip. Boy, he didn't like that. That was in our deal. He was to work during the off-season. We formed a corporation, which was Earnhardt Racing Team, Inc. The family and I, with the deal of getting him to where he could at least make a living, we always knew he would make it, but I never dreamed NASCAR would become what it is. I missed that bump by a thousand miles. We would have settled for the fact that if we could have run, paid the bills and made a living. It turned out to be a big, big thing. Everybody Dale introduced me to, no matter who was present, would say, "When my dad died, Gray had some money, and I had the ass, and we went for it." And that's about what he had to put in. Excuse the language, but that's what he would say. I was with him when he didn't have anything and his mother worked at a plant nursery to make a living. That's how far we go back. My company, Dainty Maid, was Ralph's sponsor and Dale's first sponsor. A sandwich, or vending company never advertises; they have a captive audience. I didn't need the advertisement, but it was custom then to put something on the side of the car.

Dale would go with me to Concord and he would run in that Rookie Division. That's when he drove that old pink car. He drove a bunch of them junker cars – 6-cylinders with a 2-barrel and nothing – tie the doors shut and that type thing. But I knew David Oliver, who had the pink car, and I know the man that painted the car, and I know where the paint came from. He would run those old cars like that. I ran in what's called Late Model Sportsman. He ran in that group where they gave them an hour, or thirty laps, whichever one came first. He did real well. That one year down there in Tommy Russell's car, he had won about twenty-five races that year. Randy Earnhardt married Tommy Russell's sister. Dale worked at Punch Whittaker's and various other places after we started the corporation. I helped him all I could, and he still had to struggle. If you look back, people didn't break into racing like they do today. They come in there now at twenty years of age or less and millions of dollars behind them. Look at Harry Gant. He was thirty-eight years old before he ever made it. Look at Morgan Shepherd. He was a whole lot better driver than his record shows. He was a good, tough driver when we used to run against him at Hickory. I bought the first car to put in that corporation and that's the one I think Action has come out with a die-cast of it now. NASCAR assigned us number eight because that's what we requested, that being Ralph's number. Montclair Furniture in Hickory was sponsoring Harry Gant, so he built a new car, and we bought his old one. I run into Harry every once in a while, and he calls me 'the sandwich man.' He says, "Sandwich man, I would never sell you another car." Because we took his old car and bought his used tires and outran him all year. There's no driver like a hungry driver, and Dale was hungry.

Dale wanted to go to Concord 'cause we were running for groceries and for light bills and things like that. He would want to run Concord. I would tell him no, that we were going to go to Birmingham. In other words, I'm the one trying to get sponsors, and I can't get a big sponsor if you're just going to run Concord. The only thing I could do was just get somebody in Concord. This particular night, and I later heard someone ask Richard Childress, "When's the first time you ever saw that Earnhardt kid?" He said, "Down at Caraway Speedway at Asheboro." I remember the race that he saw him in. We went down there and Butch Lindley, a good driver and national champion, was the "hot dog" down there. Dale had run him down, caught him, and cut a tire down and so he came into the pits. Randy and Danny, his brothers, put a left front on it real quick, and he went back out. He ran Butch down again. On the last lap, when they were coming off the fourth turn, Dale leaned into him. Butch was scraping the wall so it was slowing him down. Dale gets across the finish line and wins the race by a car length or less. Then when Dale goes on down to the corner and slows down, Butch comes on down there and runs all over him and tore our car up. I mean, he tore it up. So we won the race, but we lost the car. As I told him then, "They don't remember who was second."

I have to give him credit, and I've told my own children, if you give yourself two choices in life, you are going to always take the easy one." Dale Earnhardt was a good welder. He was a good painter. He was a good mechanic. He had a whole lot of talents in a lot of ways. But I never, ever, ever heard him say, "If I can't make it as a driver, I'll do this." He was single-minded, and that's what it takes. He never gave himself another choice. If you don't give yourself another choice, you don't have a choice.

Around 1977, I had a brother who was murdered down in Burlington. He went into his business, and there was a drug addict in there who had broken the back window, and as he walked past him, the addict shot him in the back. So I had to leave and try to take care of my brother's business and sell it, et cetera. It must have been 1977, and I was gone for some time. When I came back, Dale had sold everything and gone to Rod Osterlund. That would have been at the end of '78. I guess in all honesty, if I had been there, that's what I would have told him to do. That was what our goal was. Even though he was still under contract to Earnhardt Racing Team. He came to see me quite often when I lived in Mooresville. We were always going to do something together, but time runs out.

In January of '94, he told me to "Come over and spend the day with me and let's talk about this old corporation," 'cause really it ran on up into the eighties, and we had an option for another five years. Anyway, I went over and spent the day with him. Then we didn't get back together until

October. I think the things we agreed on that day must have met some opposition because of the time period. Dale owned Sports Image, which made the die-cast cars, at that time. He was going to do everything pertaining to the rookies. He was going to run one of Tommy Russell's cars. The pink car was never mentioned. He was going to run a die-cast of at least three of the cars that we had – we probably had twenty cars. It may have looked like the same old 'eight,' but it wasn't. We had some way or another of tearing them up. They were going to do that and a lot of the other rookie things. Really, that's what I've been working on.

With the determination that he had and all that, I'm sure Dale would have found someone to give him his start, but they weren't there at that time. The highway is full of guys like Larry Wallace and Haywood Plyler and a lot of other guys I could name who never made it. Ralph Earnhardt would tell you that they were drivers – they were race drivers.

And if someone were to ask me how to rank Dale, I would rank him the second best driver ever, and his dad would be first. I think he's second only to his dad. His dad was very cagey. He wouldn't have made it in today's racing. You know how independent Dale was – double that for his dad. Ralph never had a checkbook. He only worked for someone a year in his life when he drove for Cotton Owens in '61. He told me that was the most miserable year of his life because he wanted to build and run his own car. He was that independent. They were good people. Dale's from a wonderful family. They seem like a generation or two back. Your word was your bond. They were close-knit, that type of thing. I've always counted Ralph and Dale as dear friends. Dale possessed a lot of tough qualities and that's what got him where he went.

Our book is going to be "Driver on a Mission." And I know what his mission was. I think it will put a lot of other tales that I've seen written to rest because I'm going to put documents in it to prove it. Things such as the spec sheet off of Ralph's last 350 engine that he did, our 1974 NASCAR license, copies of our budget for Dale's car for the year 1974 ($47,000 plus whatever we won) and the budget for 1975, and a whole lot of other things. I quit running several years before Dale started. We tried. He was at my house one night when we lived at Mooresville. My adopted son went over to him; he would always give us a hug before he went to bed. He went over and put his arms around Dale to tell him goodnight. I heard him over there whispering, "Was my dad any good when he was racing?" I heard Dale tell him, "I'm not going to tell you he was the best I ever saw, but I'll tell you he tried harder than anybody I ever saw." I told my son I'd rather for him to have said that than anything – give it all you've got.

I hope you'll take time to read ours sometime.

In the years when we were getting started, when the season would end in November, from November 15 until, I believe our contract said – we didn't ever try to just go right down the rule by the contract, I never sent him away if he needed something. I knew that, and he knew that. He worked for Punch Whittaker during some of that time. I had a Sunoco station about a block away from Dale's house, and he worked there some. He was not lazy; there wasn't a lazy bone in his body. He would do that to try to supplement everything and to try to carry it through. It may not sound like a lot of money now, but when we paid Harry ten thousand for that car, we turned around and spent ten more on it. We had a lot in it. Then there are all the things it takes to keep it going for the season. The earnings didn't even come close to paying for it. If we would win, the highest purse would be about five hundred dollars. They would charge you twenty dollars to get in – ten dollars apiece. They called it insurance – you were supposed to be insured. Whenever you take that and you figure all the others, I still have credit cards that Dale used and that his dad used. I got his signature on a lot of things.

He went down somewhere around Cary, North Carolina one winter there when they were paying triple time for welders. He worked there, and when he came back his eyes were as red as a cherry. He went down there because he could make a whole lot in a little bit of time. I remember when he worked at Charlotte at a truck line over there fixing trailers. We just did what we had to do.

As I think back on it, I remember picking him up when he was not in school. I'd pick him up down at the arcade in Kannapolis where they were running slot cars, and he'd call me and want to know if I'd come and get him. He was probably thirteen or fourteen then. I'd go down and get him. He'd been down there playing slot cars all day. I'd take him home.

There Are Only Two Ways To Get Rich In Racing . . . Marry A Rich Girl, Or Work Your Rear End Off For 30 Years, Then Marry A Rich Girl.

Kenny Troutt

Kenny Troutt was working on Bobby Isaac's team for legendary crew chief Harry Hyde when Dale Earnhardt began in Winston Cup racing. Troutt saw Earnhardt's greatness from the beginning. Today Troutt is an instructor at the Auto Diesel College in Nashville. Over the years Earnhardt has hired his students to work on his cars.

I've first met Dale in 1970 when I came to Charlotte and started working as a fabricator and pit crewman on the K&K Insurance Dodge car team with Bobby Isaac. Then there weren't really specialized jobs; you just did it all. Dale was just a young teenager – hot rodder like we all were then, and he was racing dirt tracks there at Concord. Bobby Isaac was very close with Ralph Earnhardt, Dale's dad. As a matter of fact, Bobby contributes a lot of his successful driving techniques in his younger years to Ralph. I've heard Bobby say that.

Dale and I got to be friends, just running buddies. Occasionally I would go over to his house and help him with his second race car, a '60 or '61 Ford Falcon, a 6-cylinder. He and I traded work. He'd help me, and I'd work sometime at night on his car and I was building a street rod, a hot rod roadster, and he traded me some tires, rear tires – wide modified tires, that his dad had, to put on the back of it because then you couldn't get wide street tires. He and I just got to be friends from that. Dale married Robert Gee's daughter, Brenda, which is Dale Jr.'s and Kelly's mother. Robert Gee was a body man over at K&K Dodge so we were working together. Dale was dating Brenda at the time. From there on, we were always close. Robert Gee lived just a stone's throw from the Charlotte Motor Speedway so he actually walked to work through the woods there on Hudspeth Road where he lived. Ken Schrader owns that house now. Our shop was right there at the Simpson World at Charlotte Motor Speedway, the two back stalls. That's where the K&K car was located. Dale just raced down the road, and we would always go to the dirt track races on the weekend that Dale was racing there just to hang out when we weren't at a race someplace else.

Dale was good from the git-go. Matter of fact when Larry Rathgeb, chief engineer for Dodge-Chrysler in the early days, would come down and, of course, he was the Chrysler engineer over the Dodge team – us, and the Petty's team. When he was there with us, the Dodge team, we'd go get a bottle of wine and get in the back of a pickup truck and go to the dirt track races for entertainment at night, and he would go with us. We were sitting up on the back of Robert Gee's pickup truck in turns three and four, drinking wine, and watching the race. Of course, on the dirt track, when they would come through there, they were all out of shape. Larry, being an engineer and the genius he was for race cars, he was mumbling for himself. "There's got to be a way to take this out." He started making motions of a steering wheel back and forth. "There's got to be a way to take all this out of that."

That night at the dirt track was the birth of the Chrysler kit car. He got interested in dirt-track racing. He made a proposal to Chrysler to build this component car that you could buy from a parts book out of the Chrysler Corporation and put together. This is that Dodge Dart, that Chrysler kit car program. That was the birth of it that night. Larry got Dale Earnhardt, and Dale did all the testing for that. He chose Dale to do it. All this was off the record and behind the scenes, and most people don't even know about it. There are always problems when you build something from scratch – a program like that. It turned out to be a pretty successful piece – that Chrysler kit car. That's what started it all that night sitting on the back of a pickup truck drinking Boone's Farm wine and watching the local Saturday night dirt track races.

Dale got his first ride when Rod Osterlund was down there. I think his driver was either Dave Marcis or David Pearson, and he got hurt and had to lay out a race. The National 500 was coming up so Rod went to Humpy Wheeler and asked him who would he suggest to put in his car for his race in Charlotte. Humpy said, "Well if I had a race car, there's a young guy entered at Kannapolis locally. I believe I'd give him a shot at it." That was Dale. That was Dale's first Winston Cup race at Charlotte Motor Speedway. I'll never forget it because we were in the pits for Waltrip when I was working there with Lou, and it was his first race at a track bigger than half a mile. He was up there knocking horns with the top five just like he was part of them – first time in the car. He was running third, and I think he finished around fifth. I know he caught my eye then. We'd always been friends all along – it was great just to see him there. Of course we were racing every weekend. We were younger, crazy, partying and everything then, and we didn't take racing as seriously. Just there for a good time, but I know I noticed that day. I said, "How about Dale? He's up there running up there just like he's done this all his life." There's no doubt about it; he was definitely a natural.

In 1973, when Ralph Earnhardt died, I was in Charlotte working for a Chevrolet dealer. I dropped out when they said Chrysler was pulling out of racing. I was dating this girl pretty heavy. Harry came out into the shop and told us they had just announced they were pulling out, and he didn't know what was going to happen, whether you were going to have a job or not. He suggested that we might begin to think about getting something else to do. At that time, the girl's parents wouldn't agree to their daughter marrying a 'race carny.' I said, "Well, it's over with, so I just need to go get a real job." I was in my twenties and I just went downtown and got a job at the Chevrolet dealer to make the in-laws happy and all that stuff. Little did we know it was just getting ready to explode. We thought it was over. I still was hanging around Robert Gee's shop, and was in and out 'cause I still lived there and was part of that family.

At that time, Brenda and Dale were having problems. And I remember that Brenda made the comment that the only thing she regretted about splitting up with Dale was that his dad was such a good man, and was the only one she could relate to and talk to. That bothered her.

Then Dale was racing his own car, a Nova or something in the Sportsman Busch Series. He was just running that himself. He was around doing his thing, and I was on the road doing my thing, so we kind of got apart – not the same closeness. For a little old local country boy that fell out of high school – he built an empire.

Growing Up In Kannapolis Was More Fun Than Eatin' Watermelon In A Rent-A-Car.

Richard Sowers

Author of "Stock Car Lives" and other books

I knew Dale for more than thirty-five years. I'm from Kannapolis, too. That's how I've known Dale so long – since about 1962. So there's two NASCAR guys out of there – but only one famous, and, believe me, just one rich! Believe me.

One of the most distasteful – I really hated it – parts of a job I used to have when I was Executive Director of Public Relations at Atlanta Motor Speedway was that occasionally you had to get something autographed – helmet, flag, et cetera, by as many drivers as you could round up to give to some politician, celebrity, whatever. When that had to be done at Atlanta, I'd get somebody else to do it. But if I was out at another track or wherever, where we had to do it ourselves, I really found it distasteful. I'm not an autograph guy. I haven't been an autograph guy since I was eleven. I've got a rule of thumb. Here's where I would get an autograph. If I've got something that I think is worthy of having framed and hanging on the wall and that, that person might come over and see it. In other words, Bobby Allison is about the only autograph that I would ever get. But anyhow, I had to do that. Those guys hate doing it. I hated doing it. It was just part of the job that I detested.

One year I was at the Brickyard, and I was getting something or another autographed by a bunch of people, and Dale was surrounded by a lot of people. I said, "Dale, I need to get you to sign this." He said, "You know the rule. No autographs in the garage – period." Well, fifteen or twenty minutes later, Earnhardt comes around the corner and says, "Richard, come here a minute. Richard. I hated to have to tell you that. I was just surrounded by a bunch of people. Any time you need anything, you got it. Just don't do it when there's a bunch of people around." I said, "Well, you know I hate it as badly as you do. Believe me." But he sought me out so he could sign whatever it was – flag, I think.

I've covered Winston Cup racing off and on since 1973. Sometimes I've gone to half the races in a year. Sometimes I've gone to two or three. I probably went to fewer – two or three a year – in the early eighties when Dale was first getting started in Winston Cup races than I had in years and years and years. I went from probably fourteen or fifteen a year through-out most of the seventies to the early eighties covering the fewest. One year down at Daytona, I was working at The Sporting News and went down and was going to do a big Dale Earnhardt magazine article as well as other stuff. I get down there on about Tuesday of race week. I go to where Dale is and ten or twelve people – mostly reporters – are hanging around him. I used to know him relatively well but at that point I really hadn't talked to him in six or seven years. I didn't know if he would even remember. I went up and sort of joined the group for a little while. After about ten minutes, I asked a question. Dale paused for a second and said, "What was that question?" I repeated it. He said, "Guys, do you realize who just asked me a question?" Everybody looks around. Probably two thirds of them knew me and answered. Dale said, "You should be inter-viewing him. He should have played major league baseball. He was the best baseball player ever to come out of Kannapolis." He went on and on. I don't know if I was the best but I was pretty darn good at it. Dale was always a huge baseball fan. That really made me feel great. Dale starts telling everybody about some of my baseball exploits and even cited a sit-uation where I stole home to win a high school game.

Dale and I are roughly the same age. I probably met him in junior high or maybe even before. Dale was kind of quiet. I knew one of his sis-ters, Kathy, a lot better than I knew him. There is some high school in Long Beach, California that has produced the most NFL players. My high school, A. L. Brown High School in Kannapolis is second. No kidding. There was a guy, Haskell Stanback, I started in the same backfield with who was two years younger than me. At one time he was the Falcons all-time leading rusher. He was the first Kannapolis NFL player but there have been twenty-seven or twenty eight since 1974. Ethan Horton and Tracy Johnson are others from there. Dale's sister Kathy was a real good friend of mine. Dale dropped out of school early so we didn't run around together. He was always a huge baseball fan. He was keenly aware of me. I was a racing fan so I was keenly aware of Ralph Earnhardt's son. There were pickup yard ball games where we would play against each other when we were twelve or thirteen. This was back when a bunch of guys would just show up at the ball field. It was great – just absolutely fabulous. However, that was before the parents ruined it. When I was growing up, I played something every day. Sometimes in the summer, I played baseball for ten or eleven hours every single day. After school in the winter, there was football or basketball till dark every single day. Then once stuff started in junior high and high school, we were practicing something. Now I think it has to be organized, or kids don't play.

Kannapolis has about 40,000 people. I don't think there's a farm in the whole town. It had a great distinction all the time I was growing up. Sometimes around 1958, whenever Anaheim, California incorporated, until sometime around '84 or '85 when Kannapolis incorporated, it was the largest unincorporated city in the world. Anaheim was larger until it incorporated. I detest seeing the word 'rural' used to describe it. That makes me so mad. It's a poor, hard scrabble town. It's like just a small Pittsburgh or Birmingham.

It was really great in college. Anytime you needed to write a paper or something on anything, and the teacher found out you were from Kannapolis, you could write on that. You see a lot of these mill towns, which is a very good description of Kannapolis – at least it used to be. Here's what Kannapolis was like when Dale Earnhardt and I were growing up there. We're talking about a town of forty thousand, where one company, Cannon Mills which is now Fieldcrest Cannon and may be about to go out of business, employed the police force, the fire department, the water works – everything. It so dominated the city. There were other similar situations but all those towns were twenty five hundred people or less. This one was forty thousand. Fieldcrest merged with Cannon or bought it out, some kind of takeover, and I think it was relatively hostile about fifteen or twenty years ago. The funny this was Fieldcrest was smaller. I read an article in the Atlanta Journal Constitution business section two or three weeks ago that it is apparently now about to go out of business. At that time, there was nothing in Kannapolis except Cannon's world headquarters and cotton mill. When I was growing up, fifty two percent of all towels and sheets in the Free World were made in Kannapolis. You didn't go anywhere between six and eight in the morning, two and four in the afternoon, or ten and twelve at night because the shifts changed at seven, three and eleven. We're talking race week traffic jams – every single day except Sunday. It's not like that anymore. I don't know how many employees worked just in plant one in Cannon Mills at its peak, but it's got to be miniscule now by comparison.

A long time ago, I realized Dale had something going. His sister Kathy was a very good friend of mine in high school. I've never seen her at a race or anything all these years – not once. I used to see her ex-husband, David Oliver, a lot. He worked for a number of teams and now is a shop foreman for the '9' car. Even when I was in high school, Dale had already started driving. Someone asked me recently if it wasn't logical that someone coming up from Kannapolis would be a superstar race driver. I said, "No, not in that area." It would be much more likely now. Charlotte is the epicenter of stock car racing. It wasn't then. That is a relatively recent development in the last twenty years. Bruton Smith and Humpy Wheeler got the 'bright' idea to develop an industrial park near Charlotte Motor Speedway on excess land they had. And when they started attracting tenants, they tried to talk race teams into moving there. This was in the early eighties. They attracted a number of race teams to this industrial park. There probably are still a dozen or so there. Bill Elliott is a very good friend of mine, and we have talked about this a lot. Bill would never want to totally relocate to North Carolina. However, in this day and age, it's very difficult to compete for top-flight personnel if you're not in North Carolina because that's where ninety five percent of all Winston Cup and Busch teams are located. There's that original industrial park near Charlotte. There's one in Mooresville where there are about fifteen or so teams. There are others scattered out. In other words, guys can jump from one team to the other without having to move. It didn't use to be the case twenty years ago. The Wood brothers could be in Stuart, Virginia, which is about three and a half hours away. It is in the middle of nowhere and not easy to get to. So back in the sixties and seventies, the Wood brothers would come up with three or four good guys there in Stuart, Virginia and could have a great race team. Now it's not like they can easily attract guys from other teams. They are at a huge disadvantage because somebody would have to relocate to Stuart, Virginia. The other ninety five percent of the teams are in a twenty or twenty five-mile radius to Lowe's Motor Speedway.

I think everybody in Kannapolis and Concord and surrounding areas were keenly aware of who Ralph Earnhardt was. He totally dominated local short track racing, and of course won the 1956 Late Model Sportsman championship which is now the Busch series championship and dabbled in Winston Cup racing. It was then, and in many cases today, a whole lot easier to get your foot in the door in Winston Cup racing or any other kind of racing because of the incredible expense involved to get started. I can barely afford the car sitting in my driveway or in my garage much less a race car whereas if you are born into a racing family it's much, much easier. Knowing Dale and everything, from 1974 to 1979, I was sports editor of the Gastonia Gazette, now called the Gaston Gazette. Gastonia is a town of about sixty thousand about forty-five miles from Kannapolis. It's just on the other side of Charlotte so I was keenly aware of what was going on in our area's short tracks and how much Dale was dominating.

You look at all the success of young drivers – by young, say under thirty. Tremendous success over the past decade, headed, of course, by Jeff Gordon, but others also. There was a period in Winston Cup racing for about twelve years where there was not a single driver younger than thirty who had won two races. Think about it. Not a single driver younger than thirty who had won two races in their career – for about a dozen years. I can remember being at a press conference one time in the mid-seventies. Somebody was talking about, "Gee, where are the young drivers coming from?" Humpy made the comment that if a twenty five year old could play halfback for the Chicago Bears, a twenty five year old can drive and win Winston Cup races. I asked the question, "How about a twenty-five year old that is driving five miles from here every night and dominating like Dale Earnhardt." Humpy made the statement, "I think Dale Earnhardt is ready to drive in Winston Cup racing right now. I think he could get in a car and win." But like I say, it's opportunity. I don't think people laughed at his statement.

At one time, there were eighteen hundred short tracks in the country. Now there are weekly tracks everywhere – about seven hundred. You take a guy who dominates week after week – I mean dominates at the weekly short track at top division. Out of seven hundred tracks, that's probably the case at five hundred of them. There are two things separating those guys from Winston Cup drivers. These guys don't necessarily agree with me.

One, the incredible reflexes that go up exponentially with increased speed. It's one thing to dominate when you're driving sixty five to seventy miles an hour on a short track – a third-mile track someplace, but it's quite another at one hundred eighty. But the other thing is opportunity. Some of these guys are never remotely going to sniff an opportunity. They are never going to do it. They are never going to have the backing. There's an old saying, "If you really work hard and apply yourself, et cetera.... What a crock of s_ _t. I really believe that nobody gets anywhere without some-body giving them a chance. Nobody. It took Dale a while to get that chance, but I think he was ready four or five years before he got it.

I spent quite a bit of time with Dale, but never went hunting or fish-ing with him. Dale didn't golf either, but I do. We used to talk a lot, though. There's still a lot of Kannapolis left in me, and there was a lot of Kannapolis in him. Kannapolis has a way of implanting itself on you. That's the reason I hate hearing it called 'rural,' not that I've got anything against rural. It just isn't. It's a hard scrabble, very, very blue-collar town, mill town – a tiny Pittsburgh. I don't think anybody has ever referred to Pittsburgh as rural. My definition of rural is farmland, et cetera. There's not any in Kannapolis. In the last fifteen or so years it has gotten more up-scale and improved, but it has just miles and miles and miles of row houses – not exactly like the Baltimore row houses but it's not rural.

It made us all feel good after Dale became famous to always hear the mention of Kannapolis.

From what I understand, Dale probably went through a wild period in his early twenties, which is pretty much what I did. But during that period I hardly saw him at all. I was working, or in college, or in the Navy or at a newspaper in Virginia. But after I went to Gastonia in 1974, I did run into him on occasion. Usually I would see him at Lowe's Motor Speedway. I don't like the name change from Charlotte Motor Speedway to Lowe's Motor Speedway. We've got Phillips Arena in downtown Atlanta – that doesn't bother me a bit because it's always been Phillips arena. Ericsson Stadium in Charlotte doesn't bother me because it's always been Ericsson. Pac Bell ball park doesn't bother me a bit. Damned if I'll ever call Candlestick Park the 3Com Park. I'm not a huge fan of commercial sponsorship; however in the last twenty-five years it has been drummed into us so much that only a few will bother me. I can remember telling Humpy Wheeler years ago long before I ever went to work for Speedway Motor Sports, Inc. He and I and his wife were having dinner at a very nice restaurant in Daytona in the late eighties. He was talking about being in an era where they were writing a book on corporate sponsorship. I said, "Well, it doesn't really bother me, with several exceptions." I realize you've got to raise money, but it bothers the living h_ll out of me to hear it called the Coca Cola 600. It bothers me tremendously (this was before the Southern 500 had ever taken on Mountain Dew or Pepsi or whatever) to hear USF&G Sugar Bowl or FedEx Orange Bowl. If you've got the Peach Bowl or the Bluebonnet Bowl which no longer exists or the Fiesta Bowl, who cares, but you don't go around renaming the Sugar, Orange, Cotton and Rose Bowl. You don't go around renaming the World 600, the Daytona 500, the Indianapolis 500, or the World Series – the Toyota Masters or the Eastern Airlines Kentucky Derby. You don't rename classics. That really bothers me. If they want to sponsor a race at Martinsville or a golf tournament in Phoenix, who cares? But you don't rename classic events.

This year the Braves have replaced Bobby Cox making the Bell South Mobility call to the bull pen with a Cellular One call to the bull pen – I just can't get used to it.

This year's Daytona 500 didn't start until about 1:20. They went on and on and on with pre-race. I have my afternoon planned. I watch the Daytona 500. Then I watch the North Carolina basketball game at four o'clock and taped the rest of the race because they started it so late. I had just finished watching the race including post race, not three minutes before the phone rang. It's around seven o'clock, whereas what I'm watching happened around five o'clock. When the phone rang, a guy who used to work for me in Atlanta said, "Can you believe it?" I said, "Believe what?" I thought he meant that Michael finally won a race or something. He said, "About Earnhardt." I said, "What about him?" He said, "He's dead." I said, "Oh, don't tell me that." It just totally stunned me. It was almost like instantaneous – within three minutes, after I had watched the race. There wasn't a long pre-race wrap-up. A few things just sort of stand out and puzzle me. Darrell was immediately concerned, but he was not remotely concerned about Schrader, never mentioned Schrader. At the time I found that real odd. I found out later, Darrell had seen Schrader look in Earnhardt's car. That really concerned me at the time. Darrell almost immediately went from euphoria over Michael to deep concern over Dale – within seconds. What did he know or suspect? I've seen a lot of cars hit the wall. I've heard a lot of people say, "Boy you hit the wall, that speed, head-on, there's just no way...." I've seen tons of cars hit the wall, that angle, that speed, and the driver walk away. Tons of them. Or maybe not necessarily that speed 'cause other than Talladega and Atlanta, where else are they going that fast – nowhere, but top speed at whatever track at that angle, many, many, many times. I'd really be curious to know why Darrell was so immediately concerned. It went above and beyond the normal, "Gee we hope he's okay, et cetera."

I'm very proud of my hometown friend.

Following are some vignettes from Richard Sowers' excellent "Stock Car Racing Lives" (David Bull Publishing 602 852-9500). The first is from Jane Hogan, Renowned Track Caterer:

"Rusty Wallace calls his mother 'Mother No. 1' and me 'Mother No. 2.' I think the drivers are on the road so much they really like that, and I'm old enough that I'm not a threat to their families. Earnhardt announced one day to the press corps that I was going to make him an apple pie every time he won a race. This was news to me. Once I went to Europe and was gone for six weeks. When I got back, Earnhardt told me I owed him seven pies. He keeps track. Rusty found out I was making Earnhardt an apple pie, and he was jealous, so he wanted an apple pie. Bill Elliott likes cherry pies, so I've always made cherry for him – and banana pudding, because that's all he eats on race day. Jeff Gordon eats chocolate chip cookies. It's amazing. They've got all the money in the world, but they go silly over pies and cookies. If Earnhardt sees me coming, he'll stand on the back of the truck and start waving."

This next is from Hank Jones, a senior statesman of "souvenir sales."

"There's an interesting story on why I call him Earnhardt. When they had the Dale and Dale show (Jarrett's narrow victory in the 1993

Daytona 500), I saw Earnhardt the next race and I said, 'Dale, I prayed so hard.' I said, 'Lord, Dale has done so well at Daytona – won everything but the Daytona 500. Lord, he's really a good man. If you could let him win, it'd make him very happy.' But he told me, 'You forgot to tell the Lord which Dale. From now on, call me Earnhardt.'"

And finally, Juliet Macur who has been a Motorsports reporter for "The Orlando Sentinel."

"People don't realize how big a business NASCAR really is. Winston Cup is filled with good stories and great history. There are a lot of thrills in this sport, and the fans are great. I really admire the drivers. People put their lives on the line when they get in the car. You never know what's going to happen. You have 43 drivers in the race, so there's always a good story. There's never a weekend where you have nothing going on, which is great. I cover pro football, too, and the people in racing are incredibly accessible, more willing to talk, compared to other professional athletes."

I like the younger drivers, the Dale Earnhardt Juniors, the Elliott Sadlers. I don't think they've been distorted by the pressure yet. Ask Dale Jr. an offbeat question, and you get a huge offbeat answer that I love. Elliott is hilarious. It'll be nice to follow their careers to see if they end up being like the cranky old guys.

Who wants to talk to somebody who's cranky, anyway? They might bite your head off. You don't go up to Mark Martin or Dale Earnhardt when they're in a bad mood. I was a little embarrassed when Earnhardt won the 125 miler in the first race I covered and grabbed my credential in front of everybody to see who I was. He said, "I didn't think I'd seen you before. What's your name?" He scared the daylights out of me. I know now that's just him, but I was freaking out!

Courtesy of IMHF

A Reflective Moment Before The Race

Columbus Didn't Need Directions And Neither Did Dale

Dale Cline

*Dale Cline is the Editor of the Kannapolis Independent
Tribune. Cline, a race fan all his life, would go to the
Concord Speedway to watch Ralph Earnhardt run. When he
began as a cub reporter in 1977, he was a local sports writer.
One of the athletes who started around the same time was
Dale Earnhardt. Cline recalls Earnhardt's quick ascent from
dirt track racer to national hero.*

R alph Earnhardt was one of the stars out there. There were a hand-
ful of drivers who really stand out in my memory, and he was one
of them. He always had good equipment. His cars always ran
good. He was just a really tough driver. That was, in a lot of ways, probably the best racing I've ever seen. That was good drivers on a small dirt
track. They ran the cars that were pretty much stock cars. They were cars
that they had rebuilt out of a junk yard or bought off a car lot. They
worked on the engines, put a roll bar in them and took all the glass out and
raced them.

I met Dale at the fall race at Rockingham in 1977. He was scheduled
to drive a car that day. I'm not sure who the car owner was but that deal
fell through at the last minute. I believe Dick May offered to drive the car
for free. This wasn't a competitive car by any means but at the last minute
the car owner put Dick May in it instead of Dale Earnhardt, which I guess
made sense at the time. It sounds pretty bizarre now.

The next year I saw him again at the Charlotte race in May. He had
been driving for years at this time on the short track and what not. He actually broke in on the dirt tracks at the same Concord Speedway where his
dad had driven. This was when he was just starting to break into Winston
Cup. For the May race at Charlotte he landed a ride with a fellow named

Will Cronkite. This was a car that Will, I believe, had bought from Bud Moore, pretty good car. Dale drove it that year in the 600 and three other races that year. He did pretty well. This was his pre-rookie year. I guess the best run he had in that car that year was at Daytona. I don't remember specifically where he finished. For a guy in his pre-rookie season, he had a real good run there.

When I started to get to know him a little bit was in 1978. I'd see him at the Winston Cup races that I covered, and he was still running some of the dirt tracks around here then. I'd see him at the old Concord Speedway and Metrolina Speedway – saw him drive some races out there that year. Dale was our local guy trying to break into racing so I talked to him every time I saw him. We're a community newspaper. Any time we were covering Winston Cup racing, and he was there, he was either the story I was covering or he was at least a prominent sidebar because he was by far the strongest local story we had in those races.

Probably Dale's confidence impressed me the most. At the time it was a quiet confidence. I remember going out to interview him at Charlotte Motor Speedway, now Lowe's Motor Speedway, in May of '78. That was probably the first time I really talked to him a lot. He was out there with Will Cronkite and the car he was going to drive there. At the time, course he had his late model Sportsman car there as well. He did pretty well in the spring race in his own car, which was a Chevy Nova that he owned, that he built and maintained with him and his brothers and some friends in Kannapolis in the garage beside his mother's house, where his dad built his cars.

As far as Dale's racing operation, on the outside it looked just like all the other guys around here that were driving the dirt tracks. I think he had a truck pulling his car on a trailer. I suspect he was the only full-time employee he had. I remember interviewing him, and talking about his racing career to that point, and what he wanted to do. He said he was going to be a Winston Cup driver. I just remember how matter of fact he was about it. It wasn't like he was boasting or anything, but he was just stating a career choice just like somebody saying they were going into teaching, or going into the newspaper business. That was what he was going to do, and he was going to be successful at it.

I was at Bristol when Dale won his first year. I was pretty excited about it. Like I say, I had been covering his story as our local guy trying to break into racing and even then he had a pretty good following here. Right off the bat, he was Ralph Earnhardt's son. That gave him quite a bit of notoriety here around Concord and Kannapolis. He had already established himself very quickly. During the 1978 season, Rod Osterlund, who would be his car owner his first couple of years put him in a late-model

Sportsman car for the fall race at Charlotte. In that race, he raced Bobby Allison and guys like that, wheel to wheel, led a lot of laps, led late in the race, and finished second to Bobby by about two car lengths, which at that time was a pretty big deal. There weren't that many good cars in racing and for this guy who's a relative unknown in a race like that with the established drivers was kind of something. Osterlund put him in a car for the Atlanta race which I believe was the last race of the season in Winston Cup that year. He finished fourth in that race which was pretty amazing. He wasn't even a rookie yet, and this had been his first Winston Cup race in a good car.

The next year he goes to Daytona and raced with the leaders all day, led some laps, had some pit problems – I believe some bad pit strategy at the end. I believe he ended up finishing eighth or ninth or something like that. He could conceivably have won the Daytona 500 as a rookie had he not had those pit problems. When I went to Bristol, I didn't think it would have been bizarre for him to win that day – I didn't predict it or anything like that, but it didn't shock me to see him racing with Bobby Allison, Darrell Waltrip, Richard Petty and those guys because that's what he had done from the first time he got in a competitive car. He just stepped in and he was immediately running with those guys. I believe some good pit stops at the end of that race helped him. If I'm not mistaken, his crew got him out first the last pit stop of the race, and he held off some other drivers to win his first race.

When he came up in the press box afterwards, and you have to remember, stock car racing was not a big deal then. There weren't more than ten or twelve reporters covering that race. I suspect if you'd go to Bristol now, there'd be a hundred or more – I don't have any idea. It was just a tiny little press box, and once again, he was obviously very excited. He'd just won his first Winston Cup race, and he'd been working for years and years to get there and was finally there. That confidence was there; just like he was where he expected to be. He felt like he was there where he belonged – winning races.

Dale and I were pretty good friends. We didn't hang around together. I rarely saw him anywhere other than the track or at other race-related functions where both of us happened to be. We had a really good professional relationship, and he was just a really nice guy to work with. I never really knew The Intimidator. I guess that came along later. He was our local guy trying to break into racing. From the other side, we were his local newspaper, and he was getting a lot of publicity in our paper before everybody else caught on and realized what he was going to be.

I just know his family a little bit, and they're just the salt of the earth – working folks here in Kannapolis. They are just good solid people.

I think that's part of the connection that kept Dale Earnhardt in people's hearts so much in Kannapolis. This is a working class community. It's a changing community. Dale and I are about the same age, but we didn't know each other growing up. When we were growing up, it was very much a working-class textile community. I think people looked at Dale and could see somebody who grew up just about like all the rest of us do. And he did some pretty incredible things with his life.

I still covered racing through 1984. I covered him through his 'Rookie of the Year' year, his first championship year in 1980, a couple of lean years that followed, and then he was really starting to come back and come on strong about the time I moved into news and lost touch with him. I had a really unique look up close during a lot of the times of his career when he was breaking into racing, with his initial success, his first championship, some of the trials that followed for a couple of years. Then he came out of that and started winning again. He stayed the same guy through it all. To talk to him in the pits, coming up to a race, he was always very intense, always very focused, always ready to get in the car and get away from all the peripheral stuff that was going on. He didn't change much during that time. He went from a guy who was struggling to keep racing to a guy who was rapidly becoming very successful.

As a driver, I think one of the things that set him apart form most of his generation, most of the guys in racing now who are really great drivers came up driving go-carts. Dale came up driving half-mile dirt tracks in a full-size stock car against some pretty good short-track drivers. I don't think he ever quit being a dirt-track driver even when he was winning Daytona or Talladega – the aggressiveness. People would talk about how he would lean on other cars and kind of beat and bang his way to the front when that was what the situation called for. At Concord Speedway on a Saturday night, that was just typical racing; that was the way everybody raced. That's what he grew up watching his father in that kind of racing. When he broke into racing, that's how he learned to race, and I don't really think he ever lost that. I think it was one of the things that made him, in his generation, a unique kind of driver.

During the last few months I've seen and heard a lot of people talking about his greatest races and the most incredible thing they ever saw him do in a race car. The first World 600 to finish under the lights in 1986, Dale ran great, had some problems, got a lap down, got his lap back, was involved in a wreck with I believe Greg Sachs, that brought out a caution. NASCAR determined that he caused the wreck. They didn't want him to gain advantage so they put him back a lap down. He made his lap up again, but got a caution late in the race, maybe twenty – thirty laps to go so everybody comes in to get four tires and fill up with gas. He's the last car in the lead lap, seventh or eighth, clearly in the fastest car. I think the only question was that he had a lot of cars to pass and was there time left to do that? First lap under green, coming through three and four, he got way up against the wall, up in the gravel where you're not supposed to be able to drive, and passed two or three cars all at one time. It was just the most amazing thing I've ever seen on a race track. Passed everybody else on the next lap or two. In two or three laps, he was in first place, and he was checked out. But that was really exciting.

I saw him do a lot of incredible stuff. Some times I was there in person; sometimes I was watching on TV. That night I was there, and with that being the first Super Speedway race ever to finish under the lights and everything, that kind of driving in that kind of atmosphere, that was real excitement.

I've been in this business for twenty-four years in August. When you look back at your career and were able to chronicle just a little bit of what turned into that kind of outstanding career, it makes you realize what you stay in this business for.

Courtesy of IMHF

Courtesy of Todd Parnell

Dale Would Have Loved "Cup of Warm Spit" Day.

Todd Parnell

Todd Parnell, is the General Manager of The Kannapolis Intimidators, a Class A baseball team in the South Atlantic League, better known as the Sally League. Dale Earnhardt was a part owner of the team.

W hen our team was announced as The Intimidators, my phone lit up like a Christmas tree. For me personally, a lot of my long-time buddies called and said, "Man, this is great. This is it. You're going to be able to blow the lid off this thing now." Just the interest throughout the baseball industry was unbelievable. The people in St. Pete, where minor league baseball has its headquarters, were excited about it because of the great ownership group now. Larry Hedrick, who has been there for five years, Bruton Smith, who knows a few things about running successful sports organizations, and then you've got Dale Earnhardt, one of the most recognizable, famous sports people in the world. We had the press conference Monday after Thanksgiving. We probably didn't start seriously selling things for about three or four days. Throughout the Christmas holidays it was just a struggle to keep up with it as far as having enough products on site.

The team had been known as the Piedmont Boll Weevils, but we changed their name with the new ownership. In November, we became a team with national recognition by holding one press conference. Bruton Smith and Larry had been friends for a long time. Larry went to him because with Bruton's name, particularly in this region, with NASCAR, with Larry having been a NASCAR/Winston Cup team owner; there was just a lot of synergy there. Dale got involved in the same way – Larry had known him for a long time. Dale was born and raised in Kannapolis, actually about a mile from the ballpark. There were so many natural connections. Larry actually went over and talked to Dale about it. And he was receptive to it. Dale had not been to a game and was looking forward to it.

Larry purchased the Spartanburg Phillies in 1994 and moved them to Kannapolis where a new 4700-seat facility had been built. The team is affiliated with the White Sox. They started play here in 1995 as the Piedmont Phillies, affiliated with the Philadelphia Phillies. Then in 1996, the name was changed the Piedmont Boll Weevils and that was chosen by a 'name-the-team contest' after the first year – Boll Weevils, because of the cotton industry in this area being so huge. I came down here from Reading, Pennsylvania in October 1996. When I got here, our attendance was twelfth out of fourteen teams, averaging about 1400 fans per game. Last year we ended up ninth in attendance which isn't a tremendous jump, but it's been a steady growth all four years. We've either had an overall attendance increase or an average-fan-per-game increase. Last year I think we ended up around 1874 a game so we've increased almost 500 a game over the course of the last four years. This is like a total rebirth with the connection of Dale Earnhardt and Bruton Smith, along with Larry Hedrick. Even before the accident, with the love and adoration that the town of Kannapolis has for Dale Earnhardt it's just like a new start. It's like we've been lurking since November and starting a new franchise. Whereas some franchises move into town eighteen months before; we've basically had four months to start up a new franchise.

Intimidators is a great name. I'm not sure but I think Larry had that in his mind for some time, particularly with Dale growing up less than a mile from the ballpark.

The first day I met Dale was at our press conference. Then I saw him several times after that when I would go over to Dale Earnhardt, Inc. to have meetings with my contact over there, Dale's marketing person. Dale got involved for two reasons – the hometown connection being the first. He had been searching for ways to be more connected with Kannapolis, even though at the race track when he would get in that '3' car, they would say "from Kannapolis, North Carolina, Dale Earnhardt." Dale had already made Kannapolis a well-known name around the world. He was looking for something the residents of Kannapolis could look at as his hometown deal. We're obviously a pretty high profile item in a town this size so that was it for him. That was a logical thing. That was the first reason. It was always about the community for him. The second reason was, which really surprised a lot of people; he had a strong affinity for baseball – really loved baseball. He was a huge Atlanta Braves fan, personal friends with Bobby Cox and Ned Yost, the Braves' third base coach. He loved baseball and was excited about coming to ball games as an owner of a minor-league baseball team.

I do know that at last year's Atlanta race, he informed Bobby Cox and Ned Yost of what his intentions were here, and kind of got their input on it. There is a team in Charlotte that plays in Fort Mills, South Carolina. There are territorial guidelines, but we are both affiliated with the White Sox so it's perfect.

I was watching the Daytona race at home with the assistant general manager of the Reading Phillies, Scott Hunsicker who had come down to spend the weekend with us. We were watching the race. That's how I found out about Dale's death. Instantaneously, my phone started ringing. It was just like somebody had taken a sledgehammer and hit me as hard as they could right in the stomach. A lot of people are going to say that they had a bad feeling about it, but I grew up down here, and I've watched tons of races. My dad loves racing. There was just something about the angle at which he hit the wall that concerned me as soon as I saw it. Then it just kept getting worse. You didn't see any movement in the car; when Kenny Schrader had the reaction that he did to the medical team; when they interviewed him and he said I'm not a doctor. It all just concerned me greatly. It wasn't just the normal – oh, he crashed into the wall situation, for whatever reason.

At first we basically stopped being a baseball team. Because to the world, Dale Earnhardt, the Intimidator, had passed away. And certainly we're part of the world, but to our family here one of our three owners passed away. To us he was not only Dale Earnhardt, the worldwide known race car driver, he was one of our three owners. It was an incredibly personal situation for this franchise. We did all we could immediately to be of any help that we could be or that they wanted us to be to the family, to friends, Dale Earnhardt, Inc., and all the other businesses he owned as well. Then the city of Kannapolis came to us on Wednesday after the accident and asked us if we would host a public memorial service here at the Fieldcrest-Cannon Stadium, and we did that on Sunday night.

The place was packed. It was just a night where you have all kinds of emotions. We were working it because we had to open up the stadium. It really showed you what kind of a person Dale was because we had all kinds of people coming in. You could look at them and tell you had the blue-collar laborers who drove from Ohio for this service. First of all, the parking lot was just filled with cars from a whole bunch of states. Then you would see some people drive up in their Mercedes Benz and Lexus and know that they are doctors and lawyers and that sort. He appealed to a wide range of people and you saw that. Secondly, it was an uplifting time as family members spoke. His sisters and his son, Kerry, spoke about how he would want us to move on with our lives and in that respect we were able to aid his fans and his family and his friends in honoring and respecting him. While at the same time, I think it helped us realized that – hey, it's okay for us to get on with our baseball business now.

The program was put together by the city of Kannapolis and Mayor Ray Moss.

We have been working with the family. Their indication to us is that they are proceeding with Dale's wishes on a lot of fronts, of which this is one. The feeling there is that he was excited about this so, yes, we are moving forward. I don't know enough about it to say who will take his place as the third owner.

Courtesy of IMHF

1994
Winston Cup Champion
Dale Earnhardt

The Governor Who Didn't Use Governors On His Car

Mike Curb

Mike Curb was born in Savannah, Georgia but moved out to Compton, California as a youngster because his father, an FBI agent, was transferred there. Curb grew up in California.

I've had a lot of different experiences, but nothing like being a part of the experience with Dale. He was a very private person. Every word he said meant something. He had a look in his eyes – his eyes talked. He was a very, very bright person, in addition to being the greatest race car driver. I think you have to be bright to be a great race driver. He had the best car control in the history of the sport coupled with his intellect and his ability. Look what he's done in business. He had a real, real sense of knowing what was right, for example, the relationship with Richard Childress. Look how long that lasted. I think the secret there was that Richard was very hands-on, and so was Dale. There's no way I could have ever done that.

I had seen Dale Earnhardt race at Concord Speedway before it was going down back in the '70's. I was familiar with him and had met him when he was driving for Rod Osterlund, who was a Californian. He had driven for Rod in '79 when he won Rookie of the Year, but he had been injured, and David Pearson filled in for him and won the Southern 500 in '79 in Dale's car. I had met Dale a couple of times, and I liked him. Then I ran into him when I was the Grand Marshal for the Riverside race in January of 1980. He told me he was not sure he would be able to run the whole season because they didn't have a sponsor.

I was elected Lieutenant Governor of California in the late '70's, and then spent a year as Governor because the then-governor, Ronald Reagan, was running for President of the United States in 1980. So I was serving as Governor in 1980 and I was the honorary Grand Marshal for the Riverside Winston Cup race in 1980. 1980 was the year Riverside actually preceded Daytona, the first Riverside race.

We won Daytona, which was his 200th victory, and I brought President Ronald Reagan to Daytona to the race and arranged for it with Bill France. We won the 200th race by one foot over Cale Yarborough and this was the last victory he ever had.

"What's it going to take to be a bigger moment than winning Richard's 200th race in your own car with my friend, the President of the United States there? Or to have been the primary sponsor and to own the car that was the car Dale Earnhardt won his first championship in and to have it there in Kannapolis?" There's nothing I could ever do to top those two things.

President Ronald Reagan was there, and I had brought him there. In 1984, I was serving as his National Finance Chairman. After my term ended as lieutenant governor and acting governor, I became the National Finance Chairman for Ronald Reagan for his re-election. Reagan loved Daytona. He used to announce sprint cars when he lived in Des Moines, Iowa, as well as baseball. I have a picture of Ronald Reagan with a sprint car when he was announcing from the Des Moines Raceway. I think I saw a USAC sprint car race on TV last year from Des Moines.

After we won Daytona, we had a luncheon there in the infield. President Reagan attended it and met Dale, Bobby Allison, Cale Yarborough, Richard Childress and others. Frankly, I cannot tell you what it was like, it was amazing.

Dale Earnhardt was big in country music. He did a video with Brooks and Dunn. Most of the time when I talked with him, it was about things like that. He loved country music and knew who all the artists were.

I have Dale's car in my museum and it will always be there. In the front half of it, we've got a little museum with a lot of Dale's pictures and pictures of the car. My museum is right across the street from the restaurant where Dale's mom worked. I'll never sell it. I'll leave it there right across from where his mother worked at the restaurant right there in Kannapolis where he was born. She was very nice and seemed really young to me. Dale was good to her and took care of her right up to the end.

I waved at Dale at Daytona on Saturday, but I didn't talk to him. He was putting on his helmet to go out and do his test thing. I wish I had gone over and talked with him.

Dale Was A Chip Off
The Old Scrotum

Steve Waller

Steve is a plumber in Kannapolis, North Carolina, Dale Earnhardt's home town.

When Dale was hospitalized in traction, a little boy at the hospital was also in traction. They didn't know if the boy would live. The father contacted Dale's family and said, before the boy died, he wanted to meet Dale. It was impossible because Dale was in traction with a neck brace and rods. But they put Dale in the back of his pickup and had the boy brought to DEI. They wouldn't let anybody have cameras, but he had a picture taken with the boy and told him, "You and I are very special, so I'm going to let you have a picture with me because we're the only two people that have this neck brace." After they took the picture, they laid Dale back down in the truck and took him to the hospital. He really went out of his way for that kid. That's the type guy he was.

I go to the Speedway every race since I was a kid, and when he started winning real big, you could see the notoriety, see him on television all the time. You'd couldn't imagine a hometown guy was that big.

What Dale has done for Kannapolis is big time. Years ago, when someone would ask where I was from, I'd say Charlotte because nobody ever heard of Kannapolis. Once Dale became so popular, and they started talking about Kannapolis, I'd say, "Well, I was born and raised in Kannapolis." "Oh, that's where Dale Earnhardt's from." Exactly.

Dale offered to build his mom any size house, anywhere, but she wanted to stay in the old house. She still lives in the house Dale was born in with Ralph's shop behind it. Frankie Baskin runs a detail shop there. She loved that house, said they were raised in that house, and that's where she wanted to live.

The day of the accident, I was home with my five-day daughter watching the race with neighbors. After the race, a friend left and heard it on the radio, but it had not come on television yet. I called Frankie to see if he knew anything. He wouldn't answer his phone so I knew something was up.

One of the wildest things I heard anyone say was said by an old race fan. He said he 'cheered when Dale wrecked, and he cried when he died.' That was pretty strong.

Two Guys With Style

Steve Ellsworth

Steve owns Ellsworth Hair Designs in Kannapolis, North Carolina, and was Dale Earnhardt's personal barber.

Teresa was a customer, and then sent Dale. His mother lives two blocks from here, so he would often visit her when he got his hair cut.

I probably had more one-on-one time with him than the average person because Dale would spend thirty minutes in my chair. The last time I saw him, he seemed happy and was thrilled to go to that twenty-four hour race. He was very positive.

You've got to print this – how he was with the kids. On that TV commercial, you'd see a little kid come up to him wanting an autograph – unless he was really preoccupied at the track or something, he would stop for a kid.

He was a good guy to me and my son. I would go to the farm and cut his hair some, and my son would go fishing in his pond that he and Neil Bonnett had stocked.

I once told Dale, "You and I are two lucky people. We've got a lot in common." He looked at me and said, "What do you mean?" I said, "We both grew up here in the mill village having the bare necessities and have done better in life than either ever dreamed we'd be able to do. You're just a greater degree of wealth than me." He said, "You've got a point there."

I had this picture which says 'The Winning Cut' here in the salon, but I took it home. Dale came in the Saturday morning he won the Charlotte race on Saturday and Sunday. I said, "This is a winning cut." He was still in the Wrangler Car. I said, "You're going to win today and tomorrow." He didn't say anything; he just gave me that 'Earnhardt look.' He won, and next time he walked in the door, he had this picture. He had put on it 'The Winning Cut.' I thought that was a pretty neat story.

I saw him mature. I was riding around with him on his farm one day, and he said, "Be good to your dad. Do all you can for him. I wish I had my dad, and he could be sitting here where you're sitting right now riding around on the farm with me. He would have loved it." Right after Alan Kulwicki had passed away and then Davey Allison, I saw things change. We all do with the loss of loved ones.

Our Race Car Doubled In Value Every Time We Filled It With Gas

Tommy Russell

Tommy Russell goes all the way back with Dale Earnhardt. They began their racing careers together. Together they won local dirt track racing championships at Speed World in Charlotte and at the Concord Speedway. Russell remembers the young Dale Earnhardt. Russell, a teacher of automotive science at Northwest Cabarrus High School, over the years received donations of equipment from Earnhardt. Russell, of course, was sworn to secrecy.

I worked with Dale Earnhardt back in the '70's. His dad and my dad were friends. We were running dirt cars at these local tracks. We just got to be good friends right off. Then he started driving a dirt car for me. I just saw Dale do some things on the race track and you could tell, even in the early days, how good he was. We were good friends so it was just a natural type thing. He drove for me until his dad had a heart attack and died. Then he went back and started driving the family car.

Dale never did race against his dad because he was running in a different division than what we were, the Sportsman. We were running a division called the Semi-modified, right under the Sportsman division. We were running Ford Falcons.

Back in those days when we would race on Saturday night at Concord, their house and shop was right in Kannapolis. So usually their routine was the wives would always be at the race track - sometimes the kids and sometimes not. Usually we would go back to my dad's shop where we kept our race car and put it up 'cause it was right there in Concord. Every Saturday night we would go up to Ralph's, Dale's dad, and his mother would always fix a bunch of sandwiches and stuff. We'd sit around the table and, of course, run the race all over again. That was just a Saturday night ritual. You just went up there. It was just something that you did.

We ran a regular schedule for a championship at the Charlotte Fairgrounds on Friday nights. On Saturday nights, we ran the Concord Speedway, which is no longer here, here in town, a half-mile dirt track. And a lot of Thursday nights, we would run in another town. And sometimes on Sunday afternoons, we would go to Gastonia and race.

Sometimes we would run four or five races in a week. We won some track championships together.

I was about three or four years older than Dale. My dad ran a shop here in town. I attached a building to the side of it where we kept two cars. He was the only driver, but we had two cars. We would run one on Friday night, and the other on Saturday night. He was supposedly working at Great Dane Trucking over in Charlotte, but a lot of days he would just stay there in the shop with me. He was making - we'd pay him a percentage of what we took in on the weekends - a good salary for that time just racing. That's what he did a lot of times; he just raced. He was different from other drivers. I've had maybe five or six people drive cars for me but he was different from all of them because he had that drive about him. He knew back in those days that was what he wanted to do for a living, and he set his mind to it, and that was what he was going to do.

I guess what impressed me the most about him before he started driving for me - I don't know if you've ever been to any dirt-track races or not - but when the season starts, usually they start a race on Sunday afternoons 'cause it's not as cold as at night. The car I had was leading the race, and there was a caution flag. I think Dale was running ninth at the time. When they restarted the race, the car behind my car spun us out down the backstretch coming off the corner. Dust was everywhere. You could hardly see. Everybody was braking, trying to miss the accident. Here came that car Dale was driving at the time - running wide open - he never slowed down. Well, my car didn't bring out a caution 'cause he just spun around and kept going. Dale won the race. He had about a ninth-place car, and he won the race. I decided right then that the kid had a lot of potential.

I've got to believe that a lot of people are just naturally born to do certain things. I think he was just naturally born to drive a race car. He was that good - even in those days when he first started.

In 1973, we won both track championships at Charlotte. Speed World was what they called Charlotte. The other one was the Concord Speedway. It was the same promoter both tracks. We won both track championships that year. Some drivers we were racing against were Pat Garrison, David Oliver, and Troy Safert.

Then after that, my sister married Dale's brother, so we just kinda stayed friends throughout the years. I know when he won his first Winston Cup Championship in 1980; he took his two brothers and me to California for a week with him for the last race of the season. He won the race which was on a Saturday. He flew us to Las Vegas to spend the night and have a big time doing that. It was his first championship. We remained friends up to his death.

I'm an automotive instructor at the high school now. Dale always worked with me hiring some of my kids while they were in school to work at his place part time. I got three up there now working that he helped hire. I guess he had enough faith in me, so that when they needed someone, I picked the one I thought would do the best, and they had to go up there through the interview process. They didn't know it but they already had the job anyway. He didn't interview them; one of his employees did.

His wife at that time, Brenda, and my wife became good friends. Usually on Wednesday or Thursday nights, if we weren't racing, we would always take the girls out to eat. Brenda was his second wife, and Kerry was born from his first marriage. Then with Brenda, his second wife, Dale, Jr. and Kelly were born.

Dale's dad had quit driving and had hired somebody else because he had heart problems. When his dad died, Dale went back home and started driving those cars. The next season after that, he bought a car from Harry Gant and started running on asphalt. Sometimes I would go with him - I remember going to Martinsville, Virginia. Also I was with him at Charlotte Motor Speedway the first time he ran Sportsman Division (really Busch series).

It didn't take him long to adapt to the asphalt and to the more powerful cars. He was excellent. He didn't have the money back in those days that Harry Gant and Butch Lindley and Tommy Houston and that group had, but he did real well. One thing a lot of people don't know about Dale is that he is an excellent mechanic. He could build a car from scratch. He wasn't like a lot of drivers who can't build a car. He could do it all. He had been trained real well by his dad. I've seen him run lathes, where you cut metal, and do all the math that you had to do with that. You'd think he had a college degree in Engineering by some of the stuff he could do. It was just amazing the intelligence that he had, and business sense, too.

The only change I saw in him after he became really successful was that he just didn't have much time to do the things he wanted to do. He was busy, busy - on the go all the time. He's got a fleet of airplanes up there. He was going from here to there. Usually, since I'm off two months in the summer, I would make him give me a day in the summer, and I would just spend the whole day with him most every summer.

We would usually just hang around up at his shop. One year I was up there, and he said, he had to go down to Georgia for a dirt-track race to sign some autographs. I flew with him down there while he did that deal. One day I was up there, and we got on his helicopter and went up to

Richard Childress' shop. He had to do something about the car up there; I don't know - fix a seat or whatever, so we flew up there. It was just something like that – just to spend a little time with him. It just got to the point where he was just so busy you didn't get to see him too often. It was hard to pin him down. As far as anything changing, money never did change him in any way. He was the same person. And he never forgot his friends.

We both worked to build the car from the ground up back in those days. We didn't buy anything. Dale and I built the car. We built the engine - my dad, James, did. My dad built race cars in the forties and early fifties. He had gotten out of it, and then I got interested again. I was in the Marine Corps, and when I got out, I decided I wanted to build a car. My dad said he would help me if I didn't drive it, if I got somebody else to drive it. So that's where that all came up. I had some people drive it before Dale.

After he went to NASCAR and started running asphalt tracks, I continued to make the cars for a while. I followed him about a year later. We started running at Hickory on a regular basis on Saturday night. Glen Jarrett, Dale Jarrett's brother, was my driver there. We did it for about three or four years on the NASCAR Asphalt Circuit, and then we came back and went back to dirt track for a couple of years. It's hard when you've got the best; it's hard to ever gain that back. It was always our dream to go up bigger and bigger. He made it, and I didn't. But he sacrificed a lot of things along the way to get there.

Courtesy of IMHF

Chapter 3

Chris Economaki

Bob Jenkins

Jimmy Johnson

Benny Phillips

Tom Hurvis

Steve Saferin

Short Stories From Long Memories

Difference Between North And South? The South Is So Nice, Even Their War Was Civil.

Chris Economaki

Chris Economaki is one of the Grand Old Men of motor-sports. Beginning as a Cub reporter in the late 1930s, he climbed through the ranks until he became the Editor of Speed Sport News. He has also been a popular voice on NASCAR telecasts.

I encountered Ralph Earnhardt, Dale's father, in a race or two. We weren't pals. There was a north/south distinction there which was very clear in those days. He was a rough and tough guy, as most of the southern guys were.

I remember when Dale first started to achieve. There was a wonderful guy, Pheaton Guinn, who had a contract to promote Wrangler Jeans' involvement in the sport. Why they ever let Earnhardt go, I'll never understand. The fit was probably the best of any driver/sponsor relationship in the history of American motor sports. Wrangler Jeans was an outdoorsman's trousers at the time. Earnhardt was a cowboy, and those are cowboy pants - an ideal fit. It was a tremendously successful union, I thought. Apparently Wrangler was so tied in to Earnhardt that when he left Childress for the first time and went to Ford, he took the Wrangler sponsorship with him. It was interesting that Wrangler had that commitment, not to the owner, but to Earnhardt.

In the early days, Earnhardt wasn't the contender that he was later. When he first came up, he was a sort of 'bang you and get out of the way' kind of a guy like the older drivers were, like his dad was and some of the other dirt track drivers.

He was always a nuts and bolts guy. Once I went to his mother's home in Kannapolis where his father had kept his car, and he met me there. He really was interested in engines and chassis and shock absorbers and things of that nature rather than talk about the sport itself or his chances in it. He was an equipment guy.

I think what happened was that when he started to excel on the track, I remember being invited to dinner with him in Talladega, with Benny Phillips of The High Point Enterprise. He was sort of dragged there. This is a sort of new thing - this business of going to dinner with newspaper guys and sponsor representatives. His displeasure wasn't too evident but it was easy to see he would rather have been with other people. That was the beginning of the acceptance of the sport by the press. He was amenable. Finally he wound up gradually understanding the necessity of that modus vivendi and became quite a good interview subject.

Benny Phillips has been on crutches for most of his adult life. Earnhardt used to go out of his way to see to it that Benny went hunting with him and Neil Bonnett when they went off duck hunting and other game.

I did a lengthy interview with Dale before a Daytona 500 many years ago. He, at that time, had a guy supposedly representing him, Benny Ertel. When the lengthy interview was finished, I don't think it ever made air, Ertel said, "Well you know this is ours - this tape and stuff." And there was a big fuss between the network and Ertel, and Earnhardt sort of backed away from that discussion. He didn't care where it went. He was not publicity-oriented, but he was publicity conscious. I don't even think he was image conscious.

It's interesting to me the aftermath of his death particularly here in the south. It's so much greater than the death of a Jeff Gordon would have been. Jeff Gordon came to stock car racing from California via Indiana so he was and still is to many people an outsider. Earnhardt was 'one of us' as they say here. The south was, is and always will be different. There's some kind of stinging remembrance of the Civil War here that just won't go away - the confederate battle flags and that sort of thing. When Dale Earnhardt went, these people were deeply touched - much more so than the death of any other driver would have meant to them. He was one of them.

Bob Jenkins

Long-time ESPN announcer, current voice of Indy Racing League, born in Liberty, Indiana

Although I've seen people like Foyt and Andretti in a lot of races, I still don't believe you can compare anything they did with what goes on now. Those guys were open wheel drivers, and they did dirt, and they did pavement, and they did all kinds of race tracks; whereas Dale Earnhardt spent his entire life in stock car racing. I don't think there's any question but that Earnhardt had incredible ability. Probably he was as good at driving a race car as anyone I've ever seen; although I certainly think there were people who questioned his tactics sometimes on the race track. But that is what made him controversial and therefore played a great role in what made him be Dale Earnhardt, what made him famous, and what made him somebody that a lot of people sat up and took notice of.

I really don't understand the ongoing adulation. If I were Teresa and Dale, Jr. and other members of that family, I would throw up my hands and say 'Enough.' Let him rest in his grave. Let us remember him, but for goodness sake, let's stop this constant reminder that he is no longer with us.

My remembrances of Dale Earnhardt are just some of the races that he won, and some of the things that happened to him. I think one thing I'll always remember is his losing that Daytona 500 on the last lap of the race. I can't remember what year, but he cut a tire and lost the race. There have been a couple of races that he won that his victory celebration I will never forget. I'll just always remember him as a great race driver. Then there is all the stuff that I have heard about him. I knew he was a very kind person, and was very helpful to other people when they needed help. Those two things combined are what I'll always remember about Dale Earnhardt.

Jimmy Johnson

Jimmy Johnson for many years was the general manager of the Hendricks Motorsports juggernaut. One of his drivers is Jeff Gordon, who has worn the white hat as Earnhardt wore the black hat and who has provided a lot of competition for the number 3 car. Johnson attempts to explain why their rivalry is so intense.

At Daytona, Jeff Gordon was a green rookie nobody knew a lot about. In practice and testing, Earnhardt always seemed to work with Jeff when others might not want to race with him. Dale worked hard to stay with Jeff and show him the line. He wanted Jeff to succeed. Sure this would be good for racing, but I think that's just kind of person Earnhardt was. I think it could have been any young rookie with potential, and Earnhardt would have helped him

Dale didn't have a lot of education and but was probably one of the smartest people who ever lived in racing. An old uncle of mine used to tell me, "Don't let schooling interfere with your education." I think that applied to Dale.

Jeff is not a hunter or fisherman, but he and Dale did some business deals together in land and in a company called Chase, sportswear division. I think they each had tremendous respect for the other.

The difference in their ages helped create their different fan base. When Earnhardt started racing, people like me, red-necks, were watching racing. It was a lot different when Gordon came along. A new breed of fans came out about the time Jeff started. Obviously some female fans were attracted to Jeff because he's a very nice looking guy. Earnhardt fans were Earnhardt fans whether he was winning or losing. They disliked everybody that wasn't Earnhardt. They didn't just single out Jeff; it was Ford guys, and other Chevrolet guys, and Dodge guys. Dale's fans are very passionate and are going to pull for him - period. Then if Earnhardt had a problem or wreck, half the fans would get up and leave 'cause the race was over for them. The Gordon fans are more race fans, whereas, Earnhardt fans are just Earnhardt fans.

Junior and Childress made statements saying Earnhardt would want racing to go on, and racing will go on. France said, "We've lost heroes in sports before. We continue to persevere." We've never lost anybody with the appeal and notoriety of Earnhardt. We won't see that black '3' running around, and Earnhardt fans don't have anybody to cheer for now.

Benny Phillips

Benny Phillips is the Sports Editor of the High Point Enterprise newspaper. Phillips and Earnhardt shared a passion for hunting and fishing, and it was Phillips who Earnhardt chose to write his official autobiography.

"Look I finally found somebody with enough money to pay me to do a book on my life, and I'm putting in the contract that you're gonna write the book, or we're not going to do it." Then I talked with publishers, and we reached an agreement. The name of the book was "Dale Earnhardt Determined" and was published by UMI.

Dale's career kept him real busy and he couldn't make time to get with me. I'd say, "Dale, we've got to do that book." He'd say, "Don't worry about it. We'll get to it." Finally, I sent him a fax, "Let's just call this thing off because you don't have time. It's not my book. It's your book."

Next morning about eight, I got this call from a long lost friend I hadn't seen in a long time. "Let's get together tomorrow morning." So we get in his black pickup and ride around on his farm on a hot day in August. We pull up in the shade of a tree and sit and talk a couple of hours and ride and stop and talk and ride and stop and talk. That went on for about thirty hours or so of tapes and probably took three days at most.

We talked about everything – family, God, racing, religion. He was far more religious than most people thought. He talked about the media. His mind was focused in one direction. He said, "You know, I'd be at a race track thinking how am I going to make that car go faster? How am I gonna get through turn one, how am I going to do this, how am I going to motivate myself? Here comes a guy with a pencil and paper or a TV camera and says, "Dale, what do you think about Watkins Glen?" Dale goes, "H_ _ _ , Watkins Glen is next week. What kind of question is that? One reason I never got along with the media real well was because of the stupid questions they ask."

Da Coach,
The Great One
And The
Intimidator

Tom Hurvis

In 1968, Hurvis and a neighbor threw $2,000 on the table and started Old World Industries. A third of a century later, they're still partners, still friends and still neighbors. . . . But they didn't stand still. Old World is a former NASCAR Title Race sponsor. Hurvis is energetic, creative, fun and exciting to be around. One of his creations was 'Screaming Yellow Zonkers' back in the '70's.

In the '80s, Old World Industries hired Pheaton Guinn, who had run the racing program for Wrangler. He knew Dale Earnhardt and said he could get him to work for us for five grand. He also got Bobby Allison. I didn't know either of them, or know anything about racing, but it ended up being a fun time. We also had Wayne Gretzky and Mike Ditka.

That first year, we scheduled two commercials and since this was the first one Dale had ever done, we didn't know what to expect - also he was a tough son of a gun, and had a horrible reputation. He was scheduled to do one in the morning, with Petty doing the other that afternoon. Petty had to leave unexpectedly so Dale said he would do both. It turned out he had practiced, he was very nice and cooperative, and he did a very good job.

In '89 we sponsored a SplitFire 500 race in Dover, Delaware. We hired Dale for a ridiculous amount - only five grand. Can you imagine? Earnhardt won and it was the third biggest NASCAR race he won that first year. In Victory Lane when I awarded him the trophy, he started talking to the fans. He said, "You know these SplitFire guys are really good guys and supported me when I needed it. They are good supporters of NASCAR. You ought to welcome them." He really didn't have to do that. It was a neat thing.

GM made an offer of two and a half million so he left us, but he wrote a nice letter saying he had enjoyed working with us, but that business was business. The relationship we had with him was first class. That's what the great ones like Earnhardt and Ditka have in common: They'll do almost anything to win.

"Put Back That Big Jug Of Gatorade And Those Trojans And Buy Lottery Tickets Instead." "Why?" "Because Your Odds Would Be Better."

Steve Saferin

Steve Saferin is President of Media Drop-in Productions, Inc. of Hartford, Connecticut. Before his current position, Saferin was at ESPN helping produce the early NASCAR races. Media Drop-in develops lottery scratch-off games and sells them to lotteries around the U.S. His company was ready to kick off a multi-state lottery game involving six NASCAR drivers when the Daytona tragedy struck.

Our company obtains licensing rights to well-known entertainment properties, cultural icons, and personalities. We have about thirty-three different licenses in that regard, including six NASCAR drivers, Dale Earnhardt, Sr. and Jr., Matt Kenseth, Mark Martin, Jeff Burton and Bill Elliott.

One of the reasons we got NASCAR licenses was because we felt it would make a good product for lottery playing. There was a big crossover between lottery fans and NASCAR fans. And obviously the unprecedented popularity of NASCAR made it a logical target for us. I've also known for some time that what makes NASCAR popular are the drivers. Without the drivers, the thing wouldn't work very well. In fact, of all the drivers, the most popular one was Dale Earnhardt.

At the time of Dale's death, the game was not yet being played. The first one was going to start in April, in Delaware and I think maybe the Iowa game has started also. The last one starts in July or August. None of the tickets had been printed yet but the Iowa ones were just about ready to go on the press. For a couple of lotteries, there was a split-second decision which had to be made. In the end, everybody decided to go forward as planned. The Florida lottery was not one of the eight or nine that was going to do a game, but they considered doing a 'Dale Earnhardt only' game. They would just have four or five different Dale Earnhardt scenes, making it a sort of memorial tribute to Earnhardt. Given that it was Florida, and that's where the Daytona was, they thought it might work, but they were concerned about the potential reaction of the public. They focus-grouped the idea and their players told them they thought it was not appropriate. I think one of the reasons for that is the fury over the release of the autopsy photos. It's been tremendous, particularly in Florida, because it's Florida papers that have been trying to get them. This was right after the accident so the Florida lottery determined not to do anything for now. They are going to look at doing a game with all of the drivers later this summer.

Courtesy of IMHF

That Infectious Smile

Chapter 4

The Nascar Circuit: It's A Jungle Out There! Tarzan Told Me That

Quick Hits and Interesting Bits

The Nascar Circuit:
It's A Jungle Out There!
Tarzan Told Me That.

Dale would do things at the race track, we would be testing. . . . We were at Bristol testing one day, and the car was out, and it's running just fine. All of a sudden he shuts it off and he comes in the pit area and he said, "I think the crank shaft broke." We said, "What?" He repeated, "I think the crank shaft broke." "How do you know? Did it blow up?" "Well, it was getting ready to. Chet, see if the crank shaft didn't break." Sure enough, we looked at the engine in the car, at the front of the engine, and it was definitely broke. We said, "Man, how did you know that broke without just completely tearing this thing all to pieces?" He said, "Well, my dad used to make me drive with real thin-soled shoes on so I could feel the motor." That's just one instance. Lots of times, Dale would be in the race, Talladega – Daytona, he would be coming down the straightaway, and he'd say, "Hey, so-and-so's getting ready to blow up." We'd say, "How do you know?" He'd say, "I can smell it." He could smell it? He was that way at the track. Then we'd go fishing at the farm, and he'd go, "Those catfish are getting ready; they're coming over here because I can smell them."

—— CHOCOLATE MYERS, Goodwrench team

I remember coming in from a day of deep-sea fishing. We were both worn out and all of our lines were up. A couple marlins cleared the boat in front of us and Dale had to throw all the lines back in. Those marlins are so hard to catch, I was tired and didn't want to fool with it, but Dale never would let an opportunity pass. And, wouldn't you know – we caught one! He had a gusto for living life like no one I've ever seen or ever will see again."

—— KIX BROOKS, Singer

"I think Dale would tell you I taught him a lot of things. After a race, we always discussed racing. He always wanted to be at the front. The biggest problem I had with Dale was trying to hold him back. Let me put it this way: Back then, we had a 300-mile engine because of the weak valve springs. I'd tell Dale, 'We have 500 miles to run. You have to take it easy, sit there, ride a little, or we're not going to make it.' I'd keep calming him down all the time.

In the 70's Dale bounced between asphalt and dirt, but his bold driving style was already apparent.

Photo: IMHF

Daytona Qualifying - 1986

Mike Curb Productions was one of Dale's first sponsors. Pictured here in 1980, he went on to win his first of seven Winston Cup Champions.

Dale Earnhardt and Richard Childress in the early years.

To the victor goes the spoils
'83 Talladega 500 win.

Photo: IMHF

The PEAK Days

April 2, 1979 - Dale celebrates his first Winston Cup win in the garage behind his parent's house.

Dale's Mother, Martha

March 16, 1980 - After win at Atlanta

May 21, 1980 - Signing autograghs at a
Pontiac dealer in Kannapolis, N.C.

Atlanta - 1986 - Clinching Championship.
From left to right - Wranglers President Bob O'Dear, Dale,
Wranglers executive Pheaton Guinn and Richard Childress.

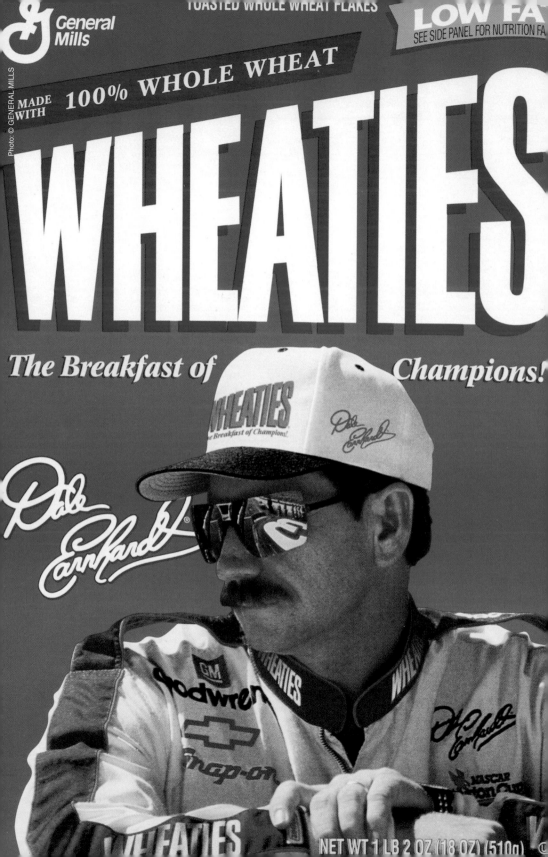

Daytona 500 win - 1998

The Winston 500 at Talladega - his final victory.

John Boy and Billy are huge racing fans. And, race drivers are huge fans of the *John Boy and Billy* program.

Dale gives some advice to Jeff Gordon and Bobby Labonte.

1996 - His biggest
little fan, daughter
Taylor Nicole

THINK PINK!

K-2

DAYBRAZU'S TUNE UP & BRAKE SER.

Dale's first ride...1956 Ford

mr

February 18, 2001 - Daytona

DODGE

April 1, 2001 - Harrah's 500, Texas Motor Speedway

Earnhardt and Rick Sturtz share a winners embrace after each winning a million bucks at Talladega.

Dale with Betty Carlan, Research Librarian at the International Motor Sports Hall Of Fame - Talladega, Alabama.

Press Conference announcing Dale Earnhardt's ownership of the Kannapolis Intimidators baseball team. Pictured with partners Bruton Smith [L] and Larry Hedrick [R]. Inset - General Manager, Todd Parnell.

Dale takes a break from the track and takes aim at a few clay pigeons.

The 24 Hours of Daytona - February 4, 2001 - 2nd place
[L-R] Andy Pilgrim, Kelly Collins, Dale, Dale Jr.

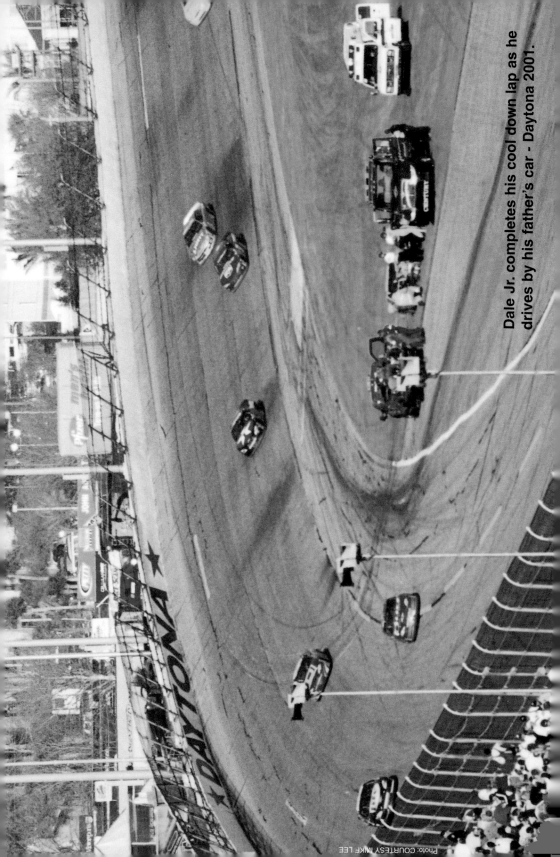

Dale Jr. completes his cool down lap as he drives by his father's car - Daytona 2001.

NASCAR Winston Cup Series

3 IN MEMORY OF A CHAMPION 3

Las Vegas - March 2001

The public memorial at Fieldcrest-Cannon Stadium, Kannapolis - February 25, 2001. Dale's son, Kerry Earnhardt, is speaking. Kerry is flanked by Dale's older sisters - Kay Earnhardt Snipes in red, and Kathy Earnhardt Watkins in black.

Relaxing on his 300-acre farm.

Rusty Wallace waves #3 flag paying tribute to Dale during his victory lap at California Motor Speedway April 29, 2001.

"I remember one time at Darlington we were leading the race. I told him, 'All right, Dale, you have to take it easy now. Slow her down a little bit.' And when he did, he started running three- or four-tenths a lap faster!' I told him, 'That's telling you one thing: you're driving too hard.' And we won the race. Sure did. Like I said, if we had the knowledge then of how to maintain the valve springs, there isn't any doubt in my mind we would have won ten races a year with Dale Earnhardt in 1982 and '83.

"I'd say in my career since 1960, I changed valve springs on our race engine every Sunday morning. I'd say me and Leonard Wood changed more valve springs than anybody in the whole circuit, and it's all because of one little problem, the solution to which we stumbled on in 1989. All it was lacking was oil. But back in '83, the valve springs were a serious problem for us, and at the end of the year Dale went back to Richard Childress. Dale was learning. I hated to lose him.

—— **BUD MOORE,** Race Team Owner

My wife is originally from Granite City, Illinois, which is right across the river from St. Louis. She lived in St. Louis for more than twenty years. She used to be a huge Cardinal fan, just like everybody in St. Louis. She was also, and still is to a certain extent, a big Rusty Wallace fan 'cause he's from there. And she thought Rusty was cute. Cute and from St. Louis – that was the combination, plus he wins a lot.

But anyhow, she's a huge Rusty Wallace fan. We were at some kind of formal thing at Lowe's Motor Speedway which I am guessing, 'cause I don't remember going to too many formal things there, it was probably the Driver of the Quarter Century dinner, or something. There was a cocktail party beforehand. Being a Rusty fan, and thinking that Dale was the dirtiest driver who ever lived, my wife hated Earnhardt. I said, "Hey. First of all Dale's a very nice guy. Secondly, he's a great, great race driver, et cetera." Well, we get to the cocktail party early and she's in the bathroom. Dale and Teresa are standing there. I knew Teresa, but not well. I never knew her well, but I've had some dealings with her. Dale said, "Where's that beautiful wife of yours? When are we ever going to meet her?" I said, "I'm not sure she wants to meet you." He said, "What's the deal?" I said, "She is a huge Rusty fan and just hates Dale Earnhardt." He said, "Well, we're going to change that." I said, "She's in the bathroom right now. Why don't you grab her when she comes out and just see what you can do about this situation." Well, she comes out of the bathroom, and Earnhardt is waiting on her. Teresa and I are standing there watching the whole thing. Dale says, "Excuse me. I understand you are afflicted." She looked at him, and she was about halfway scared to death – you know from The Intimidator, whom I never thought of as Intimidating. She said, "What do you mean?" He said, "I understand you are a Rusty Wallace fan. We have got to do something to relieve you of this disease. What can be done? I understand you don't even like Dale Earnhardt." She is just red as a beet. He just charmed the socks off of her. She has liked Dale ever since.

—— **RICHARD SOWERS,** Author, "Stock Car Lives"

I was very impressed with Earnhardt. When we brought Ditka down to NASCAR, it was a huge thing in Daytona. Ditka said, "Well, heck I want to meet Earnhardt. Anybody who makes three million – I want to meet!" It would give us some credibility by bringing Ditka down. NASCAR was falling all over themselves to say bring him down, bring him down. So we brought Ditka down to Daytona. He went into the pits. All the drivers just – he was like a magnet – came right over to him. This was right before the race and they still insisted that they see Ditka. Ditka was giving autographs. Earnhardt comes up behind Ditka, gives him a shot in the shoulder, and gives him an elbow. Ditka turns around, and they hug each other. They had never met, and you see this – these great stars, they trust each other. There's no B.S. so they can have their emotions out and they talk to each other. Like Gretzky really wanted to know what Ditka did, how his practices were, all that kind of stuff. So when we brought Gretzky in, he and Ditka, Kyle Petty and Earnhardt were just very ecstatic about working together.

—— **TOM HURVIS,** Chairman, Old World Industries

I was having lunch at one of the tracks one day, with Don Hawk, Dale's business manager who later became president of Dale Earnhardt, Inc., and Dale. I had been hearing all kinds of things about how Dale was selling about sixty percent of all the merchandise that was being sold at the trailers, at the race tracks and also in stores around the country. So I asked Don a little bit about their marketing strategy – how they dealt with things. Much to my surprise, Dale turned around – I didn't even think he had been listening to us – and he basically answered the question. He went on for about ten or fifteen minutes just giving me a lecture on marketing and demographics. I was amazed. I must have been sitting there with my mouth hanging open and Don Hawk was just sitting there with a broad smile on his face, proud as punch, like "this is my student, listen to him. He knows more than the teacher now." But that's sort of typical of Earnhardt. He was a very bright man. He didn't have school learning; he was a ninth grade dropout. He always was a little embarrassed by his lack of education, but that certainly didn't mean that he didn't have intelligence. He was very intelligent. He was well-spoken – not necessarily really great English, but he was definitely well spoken. He had a wonderful mind, especially for business. I think if you look at great athletes in any sport, and certainly including auto racing, you will see they are smart people. You don't find dumb people doing well in any sport.

—— **MIKE HARRIS,** Associated Press Writer

Every time Dale came into the shop with a hat on, he usually left it here for my son. My son's got a collection of autographed hats, like crazy. He was probably on six or seven years old when Dale gave him the first hat, and he's twenty-two years old now. He'd coming in wearing a cap, and at first I'd jiggle him out of it for Jonathan, or he'd say, "I know. Here's another cap for Jonathan."

I would cut his hair, and he would win. It was wild. We were shooting about sixty or seventy percent there those couple of years he was winning the championships. I called him one day and said, "Man you haven't been in here in six or seven weeks, and you haven't won a race. You'd better come and get your hair cut." He said, "Do you really think that'll help?" I said, "Who knows?" He said, "Well, I'll come and try." He got his hair cut, and he won. I used to give him a hard time.

—— **STEVE ELLSWORTH,** Dale's Personal Barber

I probably did the last full-fledged article on him. I sat down with him for two hours in late January or early February, and had lunch with him. He gave me a tour and I said, "Do you ever work on the cars anymore?" He said, "Yeah, but I don't tell anybody. I kind of keep them stored. I get out there and I tinker, and I just really love it." I could see all that from looking at the cars. He had like his prized possession cars out in the warehouse that he had refurbished. He just got a huge kick out of that. When he took me into his office and showed me the pictures of him and his dad working in the garage in their backyard in Kannapolis, when he showed me the picture of him racing his dad at Metrolina, you saw what the driving force behind Dale Earnhardt was. You could see it was his dad. You could see that, even though the man had died, he was still driving for him and seemed to be proving that "See, I can be a champion." Showing those pictures just opened up another side to him. It was like you were almost always unearthing layers to this man's depth. He was like, "Oh, you're going to love this. Let me show you what Teresa got me for Christmas." She got him this really cool map that was built into the wall, and the sun follows whatever time zone it's in. Then it shows you the lightness and the darkness, and it was just so neat. He took it out of the wall and showed how he had it mounted, and he was so proud of it. It was little things like that where you really saw the softer side. There was a soft side to him.

—— **LEE SPENCER,** Journalist, The Sporting News

One time Dale picked me up at the Charlotte airport, we were driving back to Kannapolis because we were going to have lunch at the restaurant where his mother was working. While we were driving, we were on a small road going toward Kannapolis. We were approaching a section in the road where a pickup truck was about to turn left in front of him. Where you would normally slow down – the pickup truck went ahead and he then cut over on the shoulder of the road and tapped him. The guy in the pickup truck probably – in other words he cut around him over onto the shoulder of the road without even braking. He kind of slid the wheel. But he had a sparkle in his eyes. He said, "It's safer to go that way than the other way." There's something about him. I saw a picture of him standing right in front of our car, which had my name on it, that won the championship in one of the magazines and he had that same sparkle in his eyes then. I have a lot of pictures of him with the car.

—— **MIKE CURB,** Curb Records

Dale and I had our moments. Where I got in trouble, and he got in trouble was in the mid-1980s at the North Wilkesboro Speedway, where he and Ricky Rudd had been going at it for the win, and on the very last lap going into the first corner, they slid into each other and crashed, and Geoffrey Bodine went on to win the race.

Well, I was working ESPN that day and in fact I was the only pit road commentator that day, and I went looking for both of them. Obviously, this was the story of the day. First and second had just taken each other out. The first one I found was Ricky Rudd, and I had learned even early on that when you get into a situation like that you ask one very simple question and you leave it up to your respondent to tell his story. My question to Rudd was, 'What happened?'

Ricky went on very briefly to say, 'It was just a racing accident. We didn't mean anything by it, and congratulations to Geoffrey Bodine.' Then we went looking for Earnhardt. We couldn't find him. Earnhardt was missing. My spotter, Jeff Probst, and I finally found out, from talking to a couple of his crew members, that Earnhardt was in his trailer. So Probst went to the side door, and I went to the back door. Earnhardt wasn't getting out without us finding him. Sure enough, here comes Jeff Probst, and he's got Earnhardt, who has changed into street clothes. Right away Neil Goldberg, the producer at the time, comes right down to me. I asked Earnhardt the same question, 'What happened?'

And Earnhardt let fly with a collection of expletives the likes of what never before or since had been spoken into my microphone. That little son of a b_ _ _ _, NASCAR ought to throw that little son of a b_ _ _ _ out. . . . ' And on and on it went.

Well, come Monday morning, no one was pleased at all at what had happened, and Earnhardt fans were all over me for quote-unquote 'stuffing a microphone in his face.' I went back later, and I replayed the tape of that broadcast, and it was in excess of six minutes between the time of the accident and the time when we interviewed him. He was in his street clothes. The lesson I learned from that, and I learned it very well, was that for Earnhardt's fans, Earnhardt can do no wrong. If something goes wrong with a television interview and Earnhardt's part of it, it will always be the announcer's fault as far as his fans are concerned.

Dale wasn't upset with the interview. He was upset with Ricky Rudd. But he was smart enough to know that he wasn't going to take the heat, that I was. He was always smarter than I was. Time after time after time I thought I'd be working on a level playing field with him, but he was just always ahead of me. I think he was ahead of all of us. The guy was brilliant. He was simply brilliant.

—— **DICK BERGGREN**, Fox Television Commentator

In '89 I was working with Al Unser Jr. at an IROC test at the Nazareth track. Michael Andretti lived near Nazareth and had driven his Lamborghini over to the track. It's one of these whompa-whompa-mobiles. It really sounded nice – throaty and just your basic Lamborghini slick Italian sports car. He parked it next to the IROC trailer and left it there. I was just standing there kind of to the side, and Dale comes out and kind of struts by this white, beautiful, shiny car and goes, "Whose piece of s_ _t is that?" Just kind of like with a wink in his voice, sorta kinda looking at it – just to stir the s_ _t – 'cause that's what he did.

It was interesting too because that day we were getting ready to go do some PR stuff. We did Regis and Kathie Lee and a couple of other things we had going on with Al. But we had gone there and Mario and Al had gotten into a big fight at Long Beach in victory lane. Al had won the race, but Mario thought he had pinched him off. Mario had to be restrained in victory lane. It was just a big old hubbub. So Al decided that day around the testing, he was going to go over and see Mario and make things right. I found out later that afternoon as we were driving over to New York, that Al had actually sat down with Dale that day and asked for his counsel. "Hey, I've got this problem with Mario. What do you think?" Dale had said, "I've been in that seat most of my career when somebody didn't like something I did driving." He said, "You make peace the best you can, and you go on, and you don't worry about it. You're good. You drive your races." I thought it was interesting that Al Unser Jr. sought the counsel of Dale Earnhardt in that manner.

—— **BOB WALTERS**, of at the Indianapolis Motor Speedway

There was an appearance many years ago. Dale was driving for Goodwrench at the time. I've forgotten the circumstance but wherever the appearance was, they needed a Master of Ceremonies, and I was asked to participate. Dale walks in with this great looking Goodwrench jacket on. It was a real snazzy looking jacket. My wife said, "Look at that jacket." She goes, "Dale, is that thing going to be for sale in the souvenir shop?" Bottom line, we walked out of the place after three hours of doing whatever it was we did. Dale takes the jacket off and just throws it at my wife. He says, "Here, I'll find myself another one. You take this one." She said, "No, I can't. I don't want to do that." He said, "Take it." She said, "No, I really can't." He said, "Take the damn jacket." And he was laughing and smiling, But my wife had just happened to say, "That's beautiful."

He just took it off his back and . . . . Kind of like the 'Mean Joe Green' Coca Cola commercial with the kid. He just did nice stuff like that. Again, you don't put that story on the air. It wasn't for edification for anybody. That's just the way he was – just a nice guy. He would sometimes go out of his way to just do something you wouldn't think his schedule would allow him to do. I think if you earned his respect and his confidence, he was comfortable in talking around you and trusted you. For those of us who traveled the circuit week-in and week-out, he trusted what you would use and what you wouldn't use. He was just a nice guy with a devilish little smile.

—— **ELI GOLD,** Television Broadcaster and NASCAR Commentator

Dale had come back to race at Concord Motor Speedway in the late '70's on a special tribute night they had set up for his dad. Dale had just run in his first Daytona 500 and had done pretty well. It caught a lot of people's eye. He was still an unknown but he was sort of the guest of honor that night and was the big draw. To be honest, I don't remember how well he did that night. I do remember that Cannon Mills, who produces big towels, had a lot of giveaway items there. After one of the deals that he did, someone gave him a big towel, and he wiped himself off. Then he turned around and just gave it to somebody in the crowd there. He said, "You might want to hold onto this. I could be famous one day." I do remember that. It wasn't said in a bragging way, kind of a joking way. This was pre-Dale Earnhardt, the legend. That was the first occasion when I got to meet Dale.

—— **DOUG RICE,** Performance Racing Network

There was one time when he and Rusty wrecked in the Winston. That was the time the fans went up and poured beer on him before he got out of the car. The driver's side was pinned up against the wall on the front stretch at Charlotte, and some of the fans went down that night and poured beer on him before he could get out of the car. It was a night race, and I'm short – like five foot four and one-half, and so when he and Rusty met each other in the garage, all the media had come up to the front and was trying to hear what they were saying. I'm so short that I just went up behind them and stuck my tape recorder up between the two of them and got everything they were saying to each other on tape. That was when Dale told Rusty, "Man, I wrecked you." They weren't angry at each other. They were just talking about the accident. That was on the Saturday of the Winston. The next Friday, which was the Friday before the 600, that was when they still had Winston Cup stuff at the track on Fridays, it was drizzling rain so there wasn't that much going on. Earnhardt was in the NASCAR hauler picking on officials. Kevin Triplett was still the PR person with NASCAR then. So Kevin and I were standing at the back of the NASCAR hauler talking. The next thing I know Dale is standing there. He looks at me and says, "You made me look bad." I said, "What did I do?" He said, "You said I wrecked Rusty." I said, "Well that's what you said." He said, "I did not." I said, "You did, too. I've got it on tape. Do you want to hear it?" He said, "No, that's okay," and turned around and walked back in the hauler.

—— **DEB WILLIAMS,** Reporter, Winston Cup Scene

After Dale dropped out of high school, he would occasionally come to baseball games. He has always loved baseball and is a huge Braves' fan. He used to come down to Braves' games a lot, like on nights off. There's a guy named Jody Davis who used to catch for the Braves who Dale befriended years ago. Then through that, Ned Yost, who is the Braves third base coach, Jeff Blauser who used to be the shortstop, Terry Pendleton who used to be the third baseman – all those guys are at Atlanta Motor Speedway every time Dale Earnhardt tunes his engine if there is no Braves conflict. You can extend it further than those guys – Bobby Cox, too. The only art work of any kind on the wall of Bobby Cox's office at Turner Field is a poster of Dale Earnhardt. You could extend it race weekend to Tom Glavine, Mark Wohlers, Chipper Jones, Steve Bedrosian, all just hang around Earnhardt all the time. Like I say, Dale used to come down and pester Ned and Bobby to sit in the dugout and help manage. He used to pester them all the time. They'd say, "It's not like racing. You can't just give somebody a 'pit pass' and get them in the dugout."

—— **RICHARD SOWERS,** Author, "Stock Car Lives"

Dale had a very interesting mix of friends. He liked people who just treated him as an average person. He was comfortable being a celebrity, but he really wanted to be just one of the guys. Therefore, he had friends who were cops, guys who did landscaping, very unusual mix of friends. I really admired that about him. He called me one night when my wife and I were watching a movie. We hadn't listened to the answering machine. My wife walked back, and I said, "Who was that?" "Oh, it was Earnhardt. He wanted to know something about buying a VCR." He wanted advice on what VCR to buy. It wasn't unusual to get a call from him. If you were in a relationship with him, you had to accept him on his terms. You couldn't force yourself on him but he would do some very kind things for people. He'd stop at a garage and say, "How's your wife? How's your mom?" He was really unusual that way. If you accepted his friendship that way, he was a great friend.

When Dale became a superstar, the hardest thing for him was how to deal with his time. There was a song called "I'm in a Hurry and I Don't Know Why." He loved that song. I did a video for his birthday one year to that song, and he loved it. The video was mostly just shots of him being busy, working on a bulldozer or fishing or running around the race track. It had a lot of different stuff.

—— **STEVE BYRNES,** Host of Totally NASCAR

Dale had a great sense of humor and liked practical jokes, especially with someone who was friends with him. He has this property in Mooresville, and there are deer all over the place. He told Neil Bonnett, "Just go back in there and go fishing." Well, it was mating season, and the male deer were going crazy. And apparently there were these deer with huge racks, and they chased Neil up a tree because their hormones were all imbalanced. Apparently Dale was just sitting back laughing his rear end off while these deer were just chasing Neil all over the property. It was a deep sense of humor. It was not superficial. He didn't make it up. It was truly in there.

—— **TOM COTTER,** SFX-Cotter Group

When you go over to see the shop, Dale Earnhardt, Inc., it will totally amaze you. I was there not long ago. I'm teaching a high performance class here now at the Nashville Auto Diesel College in Nashville, Tennessee. We have a racing motor sports program, and I'm doing that now. I've trained students and have already placed them located in a lot of the Cup teams. I was over there visiting two of my students that are at DEI now. They came through my class and have been over there less than a year, and they've already worked on a Daytona 500 team. I was over visiting with them about two weeks ago with another instructor. We went upstairs to eat lunch at the restaurant there in the facility (I didn't even know that existed since it's not open to the public – just for the employees.). It had an elevator to go up to it and had deep plush carpeting – Lobster Newburg, and all this stuff, just for lunch for the employees. It's unbelievable. I was just floored. These guys kept saying they were going to take us out to lunch. I said, "Well, I just thought we'd go to Wendy's or something, and he took me up to this place that I didn't even know existed. I was sitting there just totally – I started getting flashbacks then to just an old buddy, a running-around, beer-drinking buddy, built this. He wanted it just for his employees; it's not open to the public, and it's just a lavish restaurant. They had high-back chairs, real china and crystal. It's like something you would go to in Manhattan for a five hundred dollar dinner. This was just lunch. There have a full staff of gourmet cooks just so the employees can eat lunch there. Not quite like the old days – we would have been lucky to get a cheese and cracker and piece of chicken sitting on a creeper. Lucky if you had time to wash your hands. That hit me more than anything. I've been to so many race shops so that was no big deal, but to be sitting there having lunch and looking around at big-screen TV's showing racing movies, I said, "Man this is something." I started reminiscing then about just an old beer-drinking buddy, an old running mate. It doesn't seem like it's been that long ago. This has just happened. Something like this would usually have to go through generations and generations of families, and here in fifteen or twenty years, a relatively short period of time to create something like that from racing is amazing.

Two of our students that I have trained here were over there getting sized up for the Daytona 500 Winner's ring. I said, "I'm jealous. Here I've been doing this twenty five or thirty years, and I ain't got one of them. I trained you guys, and you get one in a year."

—— KENNY TROUTT, Instructor, Auto Diesel College, Nashville

In 1993, the summer before NASCAR officially came to Indy for the Brickyard, they had a Chevy and a Ford Cup so I made an appointment to meet Earnhardt at eight o'clock in the morning in the garage of the Speedway. I just happened to be going by Long's Bakery, which was a famous old bakery on the west side of Indianapolis. Their specialty is hot yeast donuts. So I walked into Earnhardt's garage with a dozen hot yeast donuts that were so hot the box and donuts were all stuck together. So I threw it down and slid it across the table on the bench. He said, "What's that?" I said, "That's my ticket to talk to you any time I want to for the rest of your life." He said, "What do you mean?" I had talked to him a couple of times. I didn't really know, but I knew him and he knew me professionally – one of those deals. He kind of recognized me. He opened the box up and said, "S—t, these aren't Krispy Kremes." I said, "Son, these are so much better than Krispy Kremes." I said, "You just insulted donuts by saying something like that. Don't open your mouth until you start eating these things." In the course of the hour that I interviewed him, he ate every donut – all of them. Every time I saw him after that for the next couple of years, he'd say, "Hey, where's that bakery?" I said, "I'm not going to tell you where that bakery is. That's my E-Ticket to always get in your transporter when you're in a foul mood."

—— ROBIN MILLER, ESPN.com

Two things happened one night on the media tour that made me feel like we did have a good relationship and respect for each other. It was the first time the media tour ever went to Dale Earnhardt, Inc. I'm talking about the new complex on Highway 136. We walked in and all of us are milling around. I looked up to where the balcony area is to where everybody could look down on the main museum area. When I looked up there, out of all those people, I saw him and Teresa. He saw me, and he waved. That made me feel so very, very special, that out of all that many media people, he saw me look up to where they were and from that distance he waved. And later that evening when we were doing interviews, I had reached across a couple of media people to hold my tape recorder up to him. He saw that too and reached over those media people, got my arm, and pulled me through the other reporters to where I would be right up front with my tape recorder. I know there was surprise on their faces. He just looked at them nonchalantly and said, 'She's shorter. She needs to be up front," and just kept right on going.

—— DEB WILLIAMS, Reporter, Winston Cup Scene

Then I got on the wrong side of him when he won the '87 Winston race, and he took out a couple of guys in the process, and I sent that little mailing of a crushed Goodwrench parts box, a crushed Levi Garret tobacco pack and a crushed Coors beer can which represented the sponsors on the cars he tore up enroute to winning. The crews were fighting. The fans were fighting. A year later, I sent out these items, and it brought all the anger back out again. I remember Dale and Teresa were sitting in their car, a black Corvette. I knocked on their window, and he rolled the window down, but he didn't look at me. I said, "Dale, I think you have a problem with me." He wouldn't look at me. He was hurt. I don't think he even spoke. Teresa said, "Why did you do it?" I said, "Well, this is my job, Teresa. This is something that we decided would be good for the sport and good for ticket sales, and they have been. I did it with Humpy's endorsement." Not long after that, we were buddies again.

—— TOM COTTER, of SFX-Cotter Group

He was crazy and wild. He didn't have a nickel to his name. You figured that this was just another driver – somebody who wanted to drive, but there was no way he was going to do it because he didn't have money. A lot of factory people were coming in and big-time sponsors, and he didn't have much education. There wasn't much couth to him. So I figured he might be a good weekly dirt track driver like his dad was. What you couldn't see was his determination and really the raw ability that he had, and the drive to really make it.

—— **FRANK VEHORN,** Author, "The Intimidator, The Dale Earnhardt Story"

One of those things I'll never forget, in the post race interview once, he made reference to "when I passed so and so, I saw the air on his car." – I'm just sitting there going like – "He just said he saw the air." So I raised my hand, and said, "Let me get this straight. You just said a minute ago that you could see the air on the other car." Of course he sort of got a little bit sheepish and said, "Well I didn't actually see the air." But I used that, I expounded on that because he had actually said it. H_ll, there's a reason he's so good, he can see the air. So ever since that time, a lot of other people, Richard Childress, his other car owner, have started saying about Earnhardt, "They say he can see the air." Well, I was actually the guy who said he could see the air. I made a whole column out of this notion. So in the last year or so of his life, every time they race at Daytona or Talladega, you'd hear TV commentators and other people say, "Earnhardt's the man who can see the air." I'm sure that I'll never get credit for it, but I am actually the guy who coined that.

The prevailing view is that to pass someone, you have to have someone lined up beside you. I know there was an International Race of Champions – that's what IROC stands for – which I think was at Talladega when he passed several cars. That shouldn't be possible. There are instinctive things about aerodynamics that he understood at those tracks that no one else did. He really could do things that no other driver could do. As he got older, I think maybe the edge he had back in the eighties at the normal every day track was not there anymore. I think that time took away some of that. But he was always the best at Daytona and Talladega.

—— **MONTE DUTTON,** Author, and does NASCAR This Week syndication

When I was following in another car, Dale's PR person J. R. Rhodes was telling a story but the punch line was basically – whenever they would be in Alabama, and somebody would want Dale to do something he didn't want to do, he would say he couldn't because he wanted to go turkey hunting, something that he always liked to do in Alabama. Nobody really thought that was true – that he went turkey hunting. Then when I was in the police car, and he was making chit chat with the state trooper, the guy said, "Yeah, I like to do this, and I like to do that." And Dale said, "Well, I like to go turkey hunting." Everybody started laughing. I'm still not sure he ever went turkey hunting, and that's part of the thing – that nobody really knew.

— JENNA FRYER, Associated Press Reporter

Dale had a couple of bad years there, and everybody kept saying, "he's washed up, he's washed up." I asked this person related to him, "Did you think he was going to quit?" They said, "He would quit when he felt like he wasn't competitive any more because he loved that more than he did his hunting and fishing – those were his three loves."

— STEVE ELLSWORTH, Dale's personal Barber

I went turkey hunting with Dale one time. It was phenomenal. It's probably the best experience I ever had in sixteen-seventeen years because I had the rare opportunity to see him just as a man. He didn't even talk about racing. We were in Montgomery Alabama for two days. It was funny. I had just started dating what is now my current wife. He was giving me marriage advice – relationship advice. He said, "Hey Byrnes, do you love that girl, Karen?" I said, "Well yeah, I think I do, Dale." He said, "Marry her, do it now." I mean he was just very down to earth about that. He talked about his relationships. It was just a spectacular weekend. We went out about midnight in his Blazer. There was not a light. This was about three hundred acres of nothing but wilderness. He turned the headlights off and we were flying around that farm. I was scared to death for a minute, then thought, "You know what, this guy's the greatest driver in the world." We laughed about that for years. That was a great weekend. We could see absolute nothing and he was driving across dry river beds and up hills and we were airborne a couple of times that I recall. He could just feel it. When he had a steering wheel in his hands, he felt and saw things that you and I will never see.

— STEVE BYRNES, Host of Totally NASCAR

Dale was a fierce sportsman. Joe Whitlock who is now deceased was one of Dale's first PR guys and has known Dale since he was a kid, would tell me that Dale would be sitting in a tree stand deer hunting and mosquitoes were biting, and it was hot, and he was sweating, and he had a short-sleeved shirt on, and the mosquitoes were just buzzing. He didn't want to slap the mosquitoes because that would scare away the deer. And he didn't want to put on insect repellent because they could smell the scent and be frightened off. So he would just sit there for hours being eaten up by mosquitoes. That's how focused and determined he was.

— TOM COTTER, SFX-Cotter Group

Benny Phillips has been on crutches most of his adult life. Earnhardt used to go out of his way to see to it that Benny went hunting with him and Neil Bonnett.

— CHRIS ECONOMAKI, Racing Great

You know Dale liked hunting a bunch. He took me in this one shop which had a lot of deer heads mounted. When we wee riding, he said, "Racing has really changed now. When I'm not racing, I'm doing testing. When I'm not testing, I'm doing commercials and endorsements and gone." I thought this was kind of neat what he said. He said the biggest thrill he had now is having his little daughter, about four years old at that time. He had built a tree house on the land, and he says going up into the tree house with her and sitting in the tree house in the evening and watching the deer walk around the land. That gave him a lot of joy. I was thinking to myself that was really neat. From being a wild and crazy kid to now, in his later age, a father, he thinks it's a great thing to sit in a tree stand, and not to be hunting, just to sit with his baby girl and watch the deers roaming the property. I thought it was wonderful. It showed the maturity and the change in him.

— LOU LaROSA, Famed Racer, and named "Engine Builder of the Year"

Another thing about Dale, he had incredible vision. The next morning we're driving down through this field. He said, "Look over there. Look at those turkeys." I'm going, "What are you talking about?" He was looking hundreds of yards ahead. It was incredible. His vision was phenomenal. We drove through another clearing, and he goes, "There's deer, deer, look over there." I'm squinting. He would get aggravated and point and say, "There, don't you see them?" You and I would be looking fifteen feet ahead. He was looking hundreds of yards ahead. Dale shot one turkey. Again, I never saw it. He carried it back and cleaned it up and gave it to a friend of his down there to eat.

— STEVE BYRNES, Host of Totally NASCAR

It must have been '78 or '79 when I was covering racing as sports editor for the High Point Enterprise. I did some stories on Dale. I had been covering racing since about 1962, back when his dad was racing. We just sort of hooked up. We both like hunting and fishing, and we both had lost our fathers at the time so we had that in common. It was just a relationship that kind of grew along. We've hunted and fished together for a long time.

In '79, Dale was a rookie. After the season was over that year, that winter we went fishing one day. We were out in a boat. He was so excited about racing. He said, "I made nearly thirty thousand dollars last year. Do you know how much money thirty thousand dollars is? I just can't believe it – just driving a race car, I made thirty thousand dollars." Just kind of off and on all day, he would of bring it up – and thirty thousand dollars was all the money in the world to him in 1979. In 1999 or 2000, it wouldn't have been petty cash. He was living in a small house on Lake Norman at the time.

We talked about hunting a lot, but I didn't hunt with him much. He was an absolutely excellent outdoorsman, fantastic rifleman. We did go deer hunting a few times, but I would go on a trip, and he would go on a trip. Our trails just seemed to go separate ways. He hunted in Texas and Arizona a lot. After hunting season would be Daytona, and I know we would always kind of get together and talk about our hunting experiences during the previous year.

I know from hearing him talk and hearing others talk about it that he had a rifle range on his farm that was on a power line from one hill to the next – two or three hundred yards apart. He could hit the targets he was shooting at – he would just drill the holes larger.

—— **BENNY PHILLIPS,** Sports Editor, High Point Enterprise Newspaper

Dale Earnhardt liked to fish and hunt. That was one of the things he was telling me about when we had lunch together was the fact that Taylor had gone out and gotten her first buck. He had the time to spend with her that he didn't have with the others.

—— **LEE SPENCER,** Reporter, The Sporting News

In the early years of ESPN, auto racing was really the only profitable property that the network had. It was the only property where the rights' fees were low enough, the audience was high enough, and the advertisers were willing to pay enough that you actually made money on it. I will say this that going to a race changes your opinion of it. It is a spectacle.

—— **STEVE SAFERIN,** President, Media Drop-In Productions

You could get into a conversation with Dale, and he would get very involved in the conversation. One afternoon we were talking and he said, "You know, some people love to do this and some people love to do that, but I just really love to race. I love to get right in there and be side by side

with a competitor and go at it lap after lap after lap just side by side and back and forth, and I just really, really love that. Man, that's one of the finest feelings that anybody could ever have in their life."
—— **BENNY PHILLIPS,** Sports Editor, High Point Enterprise Newspaper

Dale never wanted to be more than one thing in his life – the greatest race car driver. He never compromised. He didn't say, "Well, if I don't make it in racing, I'll do this or this or this." He only wanted to be one thing, and he focused on it – gave it one hundred percent of his attention, and was never distracted. Dale Earnhardt was able to become that great, great driver.
—— **TOM COTTER, SFX**-Cotter Group

Dale's dad was quite proud of what Dale accomplished. One year we won thirty-seven races. We were a terror. We had good cars, and Dale was a step above everybody else as far as a driver. He did real well. I wish his dad could have seen how far he went. It's unbelievable.
—— **TOMMY RUSSELL,** former Racer, High School
Instructor of Automotive Science

I never met Dale Earnhardt face to face, but this last summer I was down in Daytona. They had a story in the paper asking a number of different drivers if they were afraid of the speeds that they were starting to build up at Daytona. I got a kick out of Earnhardt's response to that. I don't have it verbatim but I can remember it pretty darn close. It was, "If these drivers are afraid of the speed, they should tie kerosene rags around their ankles so ants don't crawl up their legs and eat their candy asses."
—— —— **MIKE LEE,** Earnhardt fan

I've had a lot of different experiences, but nothing like being a part of the experience with Dale. He was a very private person. Every word he said meant something. He had a look in his eyes – his eyes talked. He was a very, very bright person, in addition to being the greatest race car driver. I think you have to be bright to be a great race driver. He had the best car control in the history of the sport coupled with his intellect and his ability. Look what he's done in business. He had a real, real sense of knowing what was right, for example, the relationship with Richard Childress. Look how long that lasted. I think the secret there was Richard was very hands-on, and so was Dale. There's no way I could have ever done that.

Our race at Daytona this year was on Saturday and we wanted to beat the traffic on Sunday so we flew home. I got home and turned on RPM 2Night and my wife and I heard that he had died. It just seemed like 'the day that racing died.' I know racing will go on. But you won't ever feel the same way about an auto race again that he's not in. You won't ever feel the same way. You'll go to the races, you'll feel the car, but part of it died. He was the premiere driver in the premiere sport. People were even putting flowers in front of my shop where the car is.

—— MIKE CURB, President of Curb Records, Car Museum Owner

A great thrill was just waiting to see where Earnhardt was on the track and waiting to see what he's going to pull out of his sleeve to get from the back to the front like he always did. Benny Parsons said you'd be on the golf course and have a radio with you if it was a Sunday if you weren't watching the race. The only thing that everybody would ask was where their favorite driver was and where was Earnhardt. They knew he would always factor into the deal. It's true. Here's a guy who could take a fifteenth place car and win with it. You hear these guys griping and moaning, and sure he griped about the car, they all do, but he could take that car – take an inferior car and turn it into a winning car. To have that kind of magic, I don't know if it will ever be matched. Some people say Kenseth has that kind of feel. He's just a racer and works with what he has, but some of these guys – I think he one time referred to them as candy asses. I just thought that was refreshing to have- he was such a bad boy – somebody who wasn't so vanilla all the time.

—— LEE SPENCER, Reporter, The Sporting News

Back in the spring race at Bristol in 1985, the first time I knew how tough Dale Earnhardt was was not for anything he did to other drivers, but how he won that race. These were 3700 pound race cars. Bristol is a bowl so all the fumes and the heat stay in there. It was not a really hot day – seems like around sixty degrees, but still like a hundred degrees in the car. What happened was in that race, his power steering broke on lap one hundred. He took the most physical track on the Winston Cup circuit, then the Grand National Circuit, and literally muscled that car around for the next 400 laps and he won the race. I thought, "Wow, now there is one tough competitor." Anybody else would have wilted. One, he was physically tough. But also, he was mentally tough. When he got out of the car he was wiped out, but he was mentally tough enough to not let his fatigue overrule his brain and do something stupid and hit the wall. At that moment, I went, "Wow, he may be the toughest guy on the circuit." It kind of reminded me at that point of today – Tiger Woods. Tiger is so mentally tough that even the mental fatigue from the pressure or whatever else, he absolutely refuses to lose, and you very rarely have that attitude in athletes. Of all the things that Earnhardt ever accomplished, that was the one that really impressed upon me, "Wow, this is one incredibly tough guy." I think it was the 1985 Valleydale 500 in Bristol. I think that was the first race that Dale won that I covered. I remember hearing on the scanners and radios that he didn't have power steering for the last 400 laps.

I interviewed him after the race. Obviously he was tired. He was happy, but he was clearly physically tired. He was as tired as I had seen him coming out of any race car. I don't remember what he said about the power steering problem, but Earnhardt was never one to let circumstances dictate his answer. Discomfort or adversity, that pertained strictly to himself, not to his car or his team, were things he was never one to make a point about. He might acknowledge it, but he would always just brush it off and move on in any answers that he gave.

Do you realize when you're running Talladega and other places, it's like a hundred and fifty degrees in that car?

—— MARK ALLEN, Producer of NASCAR on Television

Dale Earnhardt probably had as much humanity as anybody I've ever known in sports, but he didn't like to show it. He didn't like for people to know it. He truly did care. He was a very caring man. When Scott Brayton was killed at Indianapolis in 1995 – he had won the pole at the Indianapolis 500 and was killed in practice a couple of days later. His wife Becky was a friend of mine. I was in Charlotte when he died so a couple of days afterward I called her to offer my condolences. She said, "I got calls from Dale Earnhardt. We didn't even know Dale Earnhardt." He called to see if there was anything we needed. He knew I had a little girl and said, "I just don't want her to want for anything. If there's any problems, if there's anything you need, you just call me." That was amazing to me. I knew Dale for a long time. I had heard a lot of things about him like that. That was the one that came closest to home because I knew Becky so well. He was that kind of guy.

—— MIKE HARRIS, Associated Press Writer

Dale always helps the school. He donates equipment and different things that he did for us. He's kind of funny about things. He didn't ever want you to tell anybody. He would donate something, and he was always saying, "Keep it under your hat. Don't tell anybody." He's kind of funny about that. He didn't want a lot of praise for anything. I think it may have been from the way he was brought up. His dad was kind of a quiet individual and didn't seek out a lot of praise and everything. It was just the way they were brought up, I guess.

—— TOMMY RUSSELL, former Racer, High School
Instructor of Automotive Science

Here in town, Dale had the big 'Kids' Day' over at the Kannapolis Country Club. Once a year, he would line up the kids and they would come over and have fun and swim. He would go, too, and would usually bring people with him like Neil Bonnett, Brooks and Dunn, Steve Park, little bit of everybody. Once a year he would take time off, and sometimes bring the cars and everything. They'd have a big hoedown over at the Country Club. The way Dale just went out of his way for kids and other people was his best thing.

And he bought the Piedmont Boll Weevils. They were going downhill. He came in and bought them. Now everybody I talk to is going up there. Even though he's not around, they're still supporting the team.

At one time, we had a drought. Dale bought seeds, straw, hay and whatever was needed. He supplied the farmers with trucks. This is second-hand news, but I heard that whenever Hurricane Floyd hit, I'm pretty sure that Dale sent some trucks and stuff up that way.

—— STEVE WALLER, Kannapolis Plumber

One thing that tickled Dale, one of our TV stations out of Charlotte, WBTV, does a thing – Thanks to Teachers, where they come into your school and do an interview with you. They had written an article here in the local paper about Dale and me. I think that's where the TV station came up with the idea. They came over and did a piece about the kids in school, Northwest Cabarrus High School. They came and did a deal and had it on TV and everything. When the newspaper article came out with him, he called me and asked me to bring it up there because he didn't get that paper and he made me autograph it for him.

—— TOMMY RUSSELL, former Racer, High School
Instructor of Automotive Science

An item that comes to mind was eight or nine years ago. I live in Birmingham. A guy called me from the Make-a-Wish Foundation. A young boy was terminally ill and wasn't even able to go to the races because he was not able to be transported, but he just loved the races. He couldn't get to the track at Talladega but wanted to meet or at least talk to Earnhardt. So this guy from Make-a-Wish didn't know anybody other than he knew I was involved in doing the races, so he called me. I picked up the phone and called Dale at his house and explained the circumstance to him. I said, "I don't know this young man, but they called, and if you can get a moment to do so, I'm sure they would appreciate a phone call." Well my phone rang a couple of hours later, and it was this little boy's father saying that Earnhardt had called and spent over thirty minutes on the phone just talking with this kid – just shooting the breeze. Thirty minutes.

Then my phone rings again late the next afternoon. Again, it was the kid's father saying they had just received an overnight Fed-Ex with hats, jackets, shirts and cars like they had just grabbed one of everything off the shelf at their souvenir place and threw it in a carton and sent it down to Birmingham. The father was just beyond belief and the kid was so happy.

—— ELI GOLD, Television Broadcaster and NASCAR Commentator

When we did our press event to announce this whole new relationship we brought along a kid who was a cancer patient who was involved in the Make-A-Wish Foundation. One of the goals in his life was to meet Dale Earnhardt so we set this up and had a fire suit made for the kid that matched Dale Earnhardt. It was actually 'Wheaties' orange. As I recall, that was a great experience. Dale was extremely nice and very approachable and spent time talking to the kid. This was done in the winner's circle at the Atlanta Motor Speedway on a non-race day in April, about a month before the Winston Select, which is held in Charlotte. In my experience working with a lot of athletes from professional sports, some of them aren't as approachable. I had heard stories, and he was called The Intimidator so I didn't know what to expect from him, but when we began working with Dale, we found him to be a very nice person, easy to work with, very approachable. He talked to everybody and joked around. We were all amazed at the way he approached the kid – very friendly, very nice – just a terrific guy. He was The Intimidator on the race track but off the track he was just a great person.

—— GREG ZIMPRICH, Auto Racing Public Relations, General Mills

Earnhardt said he prayed a lot. He said he never prayed to win a race. "There's a lot of people in this world, and I don't think God's got time to listen to trivia like that." He prayed that everybody would be safe. He prayed for people who were sick, people who were hurt and people that I know. I went with him to a hospital once. I think it was at Daytona to a children's hospital. I didn't put it in the book I wrote. Wrangler, or one of his early sponsors, wanted him to go to a hospital to visit sick kids.

—— BENNY PHILLIPS, Sports Editor, High Point Enterprise Newspaper

Dale was wonderful to kids. He would definitely go walking up to the children and cut up with them. One day a little boy had a crew cut. He rubbed his head and said, "You think I'd look good like that? You think I need to get my hair cut like that?" It wouldn't matter how bad the week before had been or how bad the race days were, he would go right up to the kids if there were any there.

—— STEVE ELLSWORTH, Dale's Personal Barber

A lot of North Carolina country radio stations are huge NASCAR fans. They have all these drivers on there in the mornings. About a year ago, some guy was calling in about his son having apparently fallen through a manhole cover or well or something in the back yard. He was in this well for several hours before they got him out. He was kinda beaten up. It turned out he was a big Earnhardt fan, and Earnhardt heard about this. The next day he sent him a leather jacket with his name on it and all kinds of stuff.

—— MIKE FISH, CNNSI.com

Another thing that impressed me about Dale too, when he was at the Speedway, was that he would always take time for a child 'cause he loved children. In his early days he probably had his ups and downs as a dad and with his early marriages. As he got older, and when he married Teresa, he became much more settled, and was a very strong and devoted family man.

—— DOUG STAFFORD, Executive Vice President, Charlotte Motor Speedway

My first real interaction with Dale was when I was at the speedway. One of the things that really got me was that here was this guy, one tough customer, and he was a tough customer, but he had a heart of gold. If I said, "Dale, I've got some children, or a little boy or little girl, coming today from Make-A-Wish." Between every practice session, he'd come over and spend time with them, make sure they had a hat, make sure they had a shirt, tour them around the car, sit in the car. He was really, really giving of himself. It was sincere. He would come back again and again and again, and this kid might be sitting in a wheel chair, or have other problems, so I learned that there was another side to this man, not that crusty guy, but this very soft guy.

Dale did a lot of charitable things that people didn't know about because he didn't want publicity. One of his assistants told me about nine or ten years ago that the pastor at his local church there in Mooresville just went by the farm to see him because obviously Dale couldn't get to church that often. Dale said, "What are you working on, Pastor?" And he said, "Well, we're trying to raise a little money to get the parking lot paved." Dale said, "How much is it going to be?" The pastor told him about nine – ten thousand dollars. Earnhardt whipped out his checkbook, wrote him a check and said, "If you tell anybody that I gave you this check, I'll come and rip up the asphalt myself." He was very involved in the Make-A-Wish Foundation. I can't tell you how many kids I've seen him take under his wing or sit in the race car or take in the NASCAR trailer 'cause that was important for him. But he did it for the right reasons; he didn't want publicity.

—— STEVE BYRNES, Host of Totally NASCAR

We'd go to the races in a motor home. We were at the fateful Daytona race. We were in the infield, and we sort of sat around till the races were over. Then we cook and eat and let the crowd die down before we try to get out. We were down on pit row and they were interviewing Michael Waltrip and others. She and I were coming out of the infield area and walked by where the tires were, and the guys were loading tires. I said, "I want two of those tires." He said, "I can't give you any tires." I asked, "Why?" He said, "Everybody here will want some if you get any of them." I said, "Well, they don't have to know where I got them." He turned around and gave me two of Dale Earnhardt, Jr.'s tires. We were walking about a mile back to our trailer, and I was lugging two tires on my shoulder. A guy stopped us to interview us and the news had just hit the race track. Michael had not even gotten through with his interview in Victory Lane.

The people who were picking up the tires were a contract company and were not affiliated with the Earnhardts. So they wouldn't have had any information about the accident. The Earnhardt team knew what had happened fifteen or so minutes before it was leaked into the infield. The way it leaked into the infield was people with scanners monitoring phone calls, which is not a proper way to handle things. They were people who were hearing it on scanners long before anybody announced anything. Just bits and pieces of information were coming all through the infield area.

—— **NEAL BENNETT,** Former Track Owner, Big Racing Fan

My grandfather and Dale's grandfather were brothers. The original Earnhardts, the grandfathers – one of them stayed in Kentucky and the other one moved up into the Carolinas. I'm the world's largest Dodge dealer. There was a quotation going around: "Dale drove the h_ll out of them and I sold the h_ll out of them." I saw Dale occasionally, but we just never had time to make a connection. He was back on the east coast and a real busy man doing what he was doing. He was a tremendous credit to the Earnhardt name.

—— **TEX EARNHARDT,** Phoenix, Arizona, is also the number one Ford dealer in the state of Arizona and owns seven dealerships in the Valley of the Sun.

We were in Florence, South Carolina. That's where most everybody stays when they go to the Darlington Race - it's the next town over, and it's where a lot of the hotels are. I was walking through the lobby of my hotel and ran into Dale and a couple of other people there. He said, "What are you doing?" I said, "I'm going to dinner." He said, "Are you going with anybody?" I said, "No." He said, "Come on let's go." I said, "All right. Wonderful." I'd never gone out to dinner with him before. We go with a couple of other people; he always had an entourage. I offered to drive since my car was right by the door. So I'm driving along toward the restaurant going about forty miles an hour on this four-lane road – right about the speed limit. We were talking away. There was nobody around us. The road's empty. We're driving along, just chatting. I'm telling a story or something. And with no warning at all, he just reaches over and throws the car into park. I go sliding across the road, did a couple of spins and stopped in the middle of the median. He was laughing. Everybody else in the car was about to die. We all hyperventilated. He said, "That was pretty good. You kept it right on the road." I said, "Why did you do that?" He said, "I just thought I wanted to see what you did." He didn't say anything when he did it. He just had that wolfish grin of his.

I said to one of friends later on, "Does he do that often?" They said, "Yeah."

—— **MIKE HARRIS,** Associated Press Writer

It was fun to have the only book out about Earnhardt at that time in the early nineties. But he wouldn't autograph the book. He wouldn't autograph anything unless it was authorized. If a kid had a card and was waiting in line for four hours, if the card was unauthorized, he wouldn't sign it. He could be tough. You hear all the good things now. Even before he was big, he was moody. You would write something – I remember writing something when he was running for his first championship that Darrell Waltrip said, "There's no way he can win the championship." In fact most people say you've got to lose a championship before you can win one. You've never been through it. He had lost his crew chief. He got teed off at me and said I had said that. I said, "No, I didn't say it. I was just quoting what this other guy said." We had some times, but we stayed friends. I just enjoyed the type of relationship I had with him 'cause he was not necessarily my favorite driver. Everybody, assumed that because I wrote a book on him, said, "Oh, you're pulling for Earnhardt." In fact, at the party where I went to watch this 500 when he was killed, everybody there was saying, "I know who you're pulling for. You're pulling for Earnhardt." I said, "No, not necessarily."

How did I happen to write the first book on Earnhardt? I approached this publisher. I had covered racing full time for 25 to 30 years and was getting out of it. I had the time to do it, and I had all the interviews and tapes and things I had accumulated over the past ten or twelve years. I knew Dale well. And I was intrigued by how far he had come and how he had become a success. And he was a very colorful person – very, very colorful. He had a lot of crowd appeal to him. So why not? It was something I wanted to try to do – write a book, and he was a perfect subject. It took about six months since I had so much background already. I went back to three or four races and talked to people. They would say he did this to so and so, and I would check back clippings to see if it was right. So I had to go back and check a lot of things but basically I had all the background information.

I didn't know at the time that I was talking to him that I would be doing a book. At the time I did it, there really hadn't been any big stock car racing books that had done well. In fact, Jerry Bledsoe was the first one to do it because he had done a stock car racing book in the eighties, and it hadn't done real well. He said that people don't buy stock car racing books. I said, "Well, you know the sport has changed." He agreed to do it and see because he had had some publisher ask if he had any stock car books. So we did it and it did real well.

———— **FRANK VEHORN,** Author of The Intimidator, The Dale Earnhardt Story

Earnhardt was fairly famous for leaving the race track rapidly if he didn't do well. If he didn't win, you weren't going to talk to him because he was going to be gone. I once timed him after the races from the time he pulled his car into the garage until the time he drove away, I timed him in 2 minutes and 45 seconds. So he climbed out of the car, went in, changed clothes and left – less than three minutes. One time we were in Phoenix, and the Arizona Republic, the major newspaper out in Arizona, had a squadron of reporters there. They actually had one guy who was in the media center and he had a walkie-talkie contact with people. So as the laps ran down, I overheard him say, "Will you do a sidebar on Earnhardt?" I turned around and said, "Excuse me, but there's not going to be a sidebar on Earnhardt. He won't talk to anybody." The guy said, "Well, you apparently don't know we're the Arizona Republic." So I said, "Okay, just trying to help you out in your planning." When the race was over, my first priority really wasn't to my job. I went out and immediately watched to see how the Arizona Republic fared in getting this exclusive interview with Mr. Earnhardt. And I actually stood over there and watched to make sure that I knew that nobody talked to him. Sure enough, the next day they didn't have any sidebar on him. That's one of those things.

———— **MONTE DUTTON,** Author and Newspaper Reporter

I think the one thing about Earnhardt that we as journalists like is the fact that he was always a good quote. He was so powerful and such a big star; he didn't have to kowtow to what public sentiment was or political correctness or however you want to phrase it. He usually said whatever was on his mind, which is obviously very refreshing these days. He knew it; he knew he could say whatever he wanted. He was NASCAR's last link to the 'good old boys.' It was kind of like when Mario and Foyt quit Indy car racing, there wasn't anybody else.

—— ROBIN MILLER, ESPN.com and contributor to RPM 2Night

"Dale Earnhardt was one of the most determined young drivers I have ever encountered. He had the desire, the will, and the go-get-it about him to get it done. When he sat down behind that wheel, he had the talent and the driving ability to get that car around that race track. If the car didn't work, he would find one way or another to get that car around the race track. That's why he's been Winston Cup champion so many times.

—— BUD MOORE, Well-known builder of engines and cars

In 1978, the year before he won "Rookie of the Year, During practice sessions, Dale Earnhardt had his old Nova Chevrolet running weekly. Myrtle Beach Speedway then was kind of unkempt – ivy growing up and hanging over the concrete in front of the "Stretch for Training" wall, and ivy was just laying there on the track side. I noticed in practice, Dale would go up there and clip some of those leaves off, coming within an inch and a half of the wall with his car. Afterwards I went down and said, "Are they paying you extra to clip that ivy off the wall?" He just gave me that little s_ _t eating grin, and says, "You noticed that, huh?" I said, "Yeah, you're pretty accurate with that." That's the thing I remember most.

—— GREG FIELDEN, Co-author, "Total Racing Encyclopedia,"
Author of NASCAR history

Chapter 5

One Man's Family

I think that Teresa Earnhardt was fifty one percent responsible for Dale's success, in that she was more than half responsible for the success he had in business. She's a very, very sharp businesswoman. It all comes naturally. To my knowledge, she doesn't have any business training. She sticks to her guns. She drives a very hard bargain. It doesn't matter what every other driver gets, "I want Dale to get this much," and she can demand and get royalties and whatever from companies, and they have to say yes, if they want Dale Earnhardt. That will continue now even when he's gone. I'm sure she will protect his image and she's a brilliant lady – brilliant lady. Also, she definitely added a lot of stability to his life. She comes from a humble family, although her mother's from England, which is interesting, with her little twangy voice. There's some kind of culture there somewhere, and she and Dale had a very tough existence early on. They lived in a little home somewhere in suburban Charlotte, slept on a mattress on the floor and had bed sheets as curtains on the windows. She has seen both sides of life, and I admire and respect her. She was as good at her craft as he was at his.

—— TOM COTTER, SFX-Cotter Group

Teresa comes from a racing family, just like when you look at Dale Earnhardt, Jr. and Kelly Earnhardt, who their parents and grandparents are. They had one grandfather who was one of the best race car drivers in the business. Their other grandfather, Robert Gee, was one of the best fabricators and race car builders in the business. Robert Gee's daughter, Brenda, is Dale, Jr's and Kelly's mother. I think that the fact that Teresa came from a racing family and the fact that she is such an astute businesswoman gave her an up, too. I think that's the reason they worked so well together.

—— DEB WILLIAMS, Reporter, Winston Cup Scene

In both the boys, in Kerry and Dale, I've been fortunate to hang out with those two and do interviews on a more laid-back side. Kerry especially is just so much like his dad – a more innocent version. It's interesting to see the potential that these two boys have because they both have the potential to do endless things if they just have the right people behind them. Junior does. Junior will do well. I worry about Kerry from time to time; I just hope somebody's looking out for him because he's a great kid.

—— LEE SPENCER, Reporter, The Sporting News

Teresa has been part of it for a long time. She admired and adored Dale Earnhardt when she was a fourteen year old girl. This is the only man that's ever meant anything to her in her whole life. Her uncle is Tommy Houston, another racer.

—— **TOM COTTER, SFX**-Cotter Group

I think what a lot of people don't realize is that when Teresa came into his life in the early eighties, she is the one that was very, very instrumental in that empire becoming so well off financially. She is a very astute businesswoman. They were partners, not only in marriage, but business as well – they were true partners.

—— **DEB WILLIAMS,** Reporter, Winston Cup Scene

I think things really started to change for him when he got married for the third time. This was to Teresa, and she had a very settling influence on him. He began to grow as a person, as a cause celebre so to speak, and he found out what so many celebrities find out – that's it's perfectly okay and even good to be yourself.

—— **HUMPY WHEELER,** President, Lowe's Motor Speedway

Dale always said, "I'm just as proud of my family, of all my family, as I am of my racing career." He felt that way about his mother, brothers and sisters, as well as his two sons and daughters and wife.

—— **BENNY PHILLIPS,** Sports Editor, High Point Enterprise Newspaper

I know the first interview I ever did with Teresa was actually what gave me a great deal more insight into Dale. The first thing she mentioned that he had a much bigger heart, and a softer heart, than people realized. Then of course, as I met his mother and interviewed her and interviewed Kerry and Dale, Jr., and Kelly when they were driving late model stocks, then I came to understand the family a lot more and I understood his personality a lot more. I could see why, in some instances, he was aloof, why he didn't necessarily have the time that you thought he should have. How he was able to balance everything and a little bit more while the persona he had developed.

—— **DEB WILLIAMS,** Reporter, Winston Cup Scene

In talking about Taylor Nicole, it was really neat because here's a guy who could get his daughter anything and pretty much did. He spent an entire year scrounging the country for the perfect gift for her and what he wanted to give her was a vintage Corvette from 1988, the year she was born. I don't know precisely what anniversary that is of the Corvette, I think the 35th, but he finally found it in Pennsylvania. Somebody had garaged it, and it only had like 16,000 miles on it. He had given it to her right after her birthday. Taylor told Teresa on the way home "You know, mom, I had a dream last night that daddy got me a car." Teresa goes, "No, that's unbelievable." Then when they got back to the shop, here was this car waiting for her – this vintage 1988 white Corvette. Like I said, here's a guy who could have had one of his guys do it, but he spent the time – it took an entire year – to find this car for her so it would be ready for her twelfth birthday. Then he let her drive it out on the farm. He liked to brag over the fact that he let her into the showroom and she backed it perfectly into the spot. The car couldn't have been eighteen inches from a glass wall that went to one of the offices behind her.

—— **LEE SPENCER,** Reporter, The Sporting News

"I've also gotten to know Dale, Jr. Shoot, yeah, and Kerry and Kelly. I know the whole family. I have fed Dale, Jr. They are just folks. Martha and I sit and gossip. We're just friends, like I would be friends with anybody else. They are great. I love them.

—— **BETTY CARLAN,** Motorsports Hall of Fame

Dale talked about Dale, Jr. There was a while there when Dale had just gotten to the point where he was bombarded with questions about Dale, Jr. The ego kind of kicked in there for a while, and he just got pretty gruff one time and said, "Hey, I just don't even want to talk about it anymore." Then once Junior got into the series and was winning, the love that you could see that he had for his son in eyes was just absolutely incredible. Then when the three of them were together he and Kerry and Dale at Michigan, it was a beautiful thing to behold. At that point, Earnhardt was just so comfortable with who he was and where he was and his life. He just really enjoyed being the father he didn't have time to be when he was building his empire.

—— **LEE SPENCER,** Reporter, The Sporting News

It's very, very tough. It is very emotional. It's not so tough for the drivers. It's real tough for their families. My daughter has been walking around here, and my son has been floating around, and my wife - those are the people who have to suffer each time. I remember a segment of Dale actually giving Teresa a kiss goodbye. You never knew that was going to be the last kiss that he would have given to Teresa. But there again, the sport is very dangerous, and we do everything we can to make it as safe as we can.

—— **ERNIE IRVAN,** Friend and Driver

I spent time with Dale's mother in the house he grew up in, in the living room. Martha, his mother, is a great lady. She said, "I think he was a Boy Scout for a little while. But he's like a normal kid. He got in trouble. But he was honest – hard working, focused on racing." He once told his parents he wanted to quit school. She and Ralph sat down and said, "Look, if you stay in school, we'll buy you a new car." He said, "I don't want a new car. I want to race." And he quit school.

—— **TOM COTTER**, SFX-Cotter Group

Because with him and Teresa, Teresa was the image-maker. She kind of took the image and molded the image and perfected the image and to have Dale Earnhardt without the mustache would kind of tarnished the image they had set up initially.

—— **LEE SPENCER**, Reporter, The Sporting News

Dale wanted to build a house for his mother, Martha, but she wanted to stay in the house in Kannapolis where she and Ralph lived, where they raised their children. To her that was home. I thought that said a lot about her as far as being a down-to-earth person who didn't let Dale's success take her away from her values. It's a very simple, modest house. I think it's something that maybe a lot of people would not understand – why she wanted to stay there. It was home. You have a very homey feeling there as soon as you walk up on the front porch. It's very, very homey.

—— **DEB WILLIAMS**, Reporter, Winston Cup Scene

Junior has told some great stories. He's been running stories in Winston Cup Scene and on ESPN on-line. There was one the other day where he was telling about his father teaching him how to ski on Lake Norman. It just sounds like the way my father taught me how. I can see that German influence. It's like my father teaching me how to ride the bike – put you on top of the hill and just letting you go!   That was kind of how his father taught him how to water ski was just putting him in the lake and had a truck pulling out on a boat ramp to pull him up. He said he got scraped all up and I can see this. I think that's part of the problem. I saw my father in Dale Earnhardt.

—— **LEE SPENCER**, Reporter, The Sporting News

I got asked to design the paint schemes when his children, Dale, Jr., Kelly and Kerry ran their late-model stock cars. They had me do that stuff. He kept me very, very busy, and he always kept me on my toes.

—— **SAM BASS**, Artist

Ralph also used to run down here. Kerry ran here, and Kelly ran weekly.

Kelly is no longer running. She is married, and I think she does some PR thing. Kerry is doing some ARCA stuff, maybe some Busch stuff. He was in one Cup race last year in Michigan and crashed out early.

—— GREG FIELDEN, Author

Kerry won in ARCA, and his Busch teams won in their series. It was just like he had guys winning across the board and he was so proud of what he had accomplished. His daughter Kelly had just given birth to a grandbaby and he just glowed when he talked about the grandbaby and it was a beautiful thing to watch.

—— LEE SPENCER, Reporter, The Sporting News

It was interesting because when Teresa walked up on stage at the funeral service, the first thought that came to my mind, she reminded me of Jacqueline Kennedy. When I talked to mom that night, mom said the very same thing before I even brought it up. Mother said, "You know, the way she's handling herself reminds me of Jackie Kennedy." I said, "Yeah, mom, that's what she reminded me of, too. When she was escorted up on stage by the highway patrolman, and by the way she blew the kiss at everybody and said 'thank you.' It reminded me of the graciousness that Jackie Kennedy showed when she had to go through all that with President Kennedy."

—— DEB WILLIAMS, Reporter, Winston Cup Scene

I went to the memorial service, but not the funeral. There were a lot of broken hearts in there. It was nice. It was short. His widow, Teresa, did a fabulous job of conveying her thanks to the friends who surrounded her at that point. What's happened to her since then, I think she's a hero for going out and fighting for her husband.

—— LEE SPENCER, Reporter, The Sporting News

Chapter 6

Lee Spencer

Mike Harris

Monte Dutton

Deb Williams

The Write Stuff

The Sporting News – The Best Kept Secret In Sports

Lee Spencer

You gotta like a gal who talks about scarfin' down hot dogs and "cherry seats" in the left field bleachers. Lee grew up in St. Louis rooting for the baseball Cardinals. Even though she has covered NASCAR the last seven years from her Carolina home, she still has Cardinal season tickets. She is the ace auto-racing reporter for The Sporting News.

Dale Earnhardt loved the hot dogs at Martinsville, but if anyone caught him, he begged them not to tell his wife, Teresa, that he was scarfing on junk food. There's a joke that what they dyed the dogs with was something the federal government had outlawed years ago. Martinsville red should be a color in a box of crayons 'cause there's no way to describe the color. He didn't want his wife to know he was sneaking one. She was always on him to watch his health. That was something he could sneak and not get into too much trouble over.

The first time I met him was kind of strange. Chevy had been running Luminas for a long time. They changed over to Monte Carlos and he had just come off the track from practicing, and I waited kind of diligently because you are always on 'Dale time.' I went up and said, "I heard you tested the new Monte Carlos last week. How did it run?" Well, he just grabbed my hand and started walking through the garage swinging my hand back and forth like a couple of teenagers would at the mall. I was scared to death that his wife would see us. I said, "Come on, this is ridiculous. Just please tell me how did you like the new Monte Carlo?" He just winked, and squeezed my hand and walked away. I was thinking, "Thank God his wife is not in eye-shot because she would probably have a shotgun." From the beginning, there was just this air of mystique about this guy. You just couldn't describe it. It was just the strangest thing.

The second time, I actually had an interview with him at the track in his trailer. The one thing I remember was the fact that he came out and took my hand like just a perfect gentleman and helped me up the stairs of his transporter. I thought this was really strange. Here's this bad athlete and he's being a complete gentleman putting his hand out for a lady. I thought that was just incredible.

My youngest son and his daughter are in the same grade in school. He was ahead of me in carpool line one time, and he had driven Taylor Nicole to school and he was sitting really low in this black Corvette. I came barreling in behind him and slammed on the brakes just to kind of give him a shock because he was The Intimidator. He was always a very considerate on-the-road kind of driver. This amazed me.

I thought it was just so cool that the Tuesday after he got home from the Rolex 24; he was driving his daughter to school – just spending quality time with her. If you asked him what he drove, he would tell you a black pickup truck. He didn't want to convey the fact that here he was driving Corvettes. But he loved Corvettes and before he died, he had ordered a duplicate Corvette, similar to the one he and Junior drove in the Rolex 24 to put in his showroom at the shop.

He had given Taylor a vintage Corvette for her birthday, and when we went on the ski trip, with the kids' school, I asked her about it. She thought that was pretty cool.

He had really reached, not only the pinnacle of the sport when he died, the pinnacle of being a human being. If you can imagine having no cares and just enjoying life, so satisfied with everything around you. He had built his own incredible teams with DEI. As successful as DEI has been in the last two years, nobody had enjoyed that kind of success. I can remember they had a press conference the week after Talladega, the fall race he won. I think it was the tenth time he had won there. I don't even remember what the press conference was at this point, but he walked in and he puts his arm around me and just kind of winked, "So, what do you think?" He was so proud of that win – coming back from 18th or wherever he had been to pull it off and get his tenth victory. He was still craving approval at that point – almost like a boy looking to his mother for approval. It was so incredible. Here's somebody who is just so self-assured and he still wants approval. It was so cool.

At Daytona the day of his passing, it was just one of those situations where nothing could prepare you for what was going to happen. We were out covering the big wreck that took out half the field. Quite frankly, it looked like a war zone. You had wreckers bringing in carnage from every direction. I had talked to his driver, Steve Park, and he was just absolutely livid 'cause he thought he had a car that could win. These guys were out there just walking wounded – in a daze. They couldn't believe what had happened – how fast it had happened. So once we got closed, we went back into the media center. You're sitting there waiting for everything to unfold and you're waiting for the end and all of a sudden the race takes off. You're watching what's going on. You're really not expecting the wreck when it happens. Obviously when it happens, it happens so quickly. Earnhardt's caught in a wreck. But Michael Waltrip's going on; he's going to get his first win which is going to be a heck of a story, especially with Earnhardt holding off the field – although that's been debated. There are the doubters but I think it was an act of selflessness. To watch what unfolded and to see the wreck, you're thinking, "Hey, it was just a wreck." I called my girlfriend who is Tony Stewart's manager and she's at the hospital. She's just very grave when I called. I'm thinking, "This isn't good. Maybe Tony's worse off than we thought," thinking that Earnhardt was indestructible. No one thought Earnhardt was destructible. Several hours after he has been at the hospital, people are coming in and saying, "He's dead. He's dead." At this point to me, it's just completely speculation. I had so much doubt I cannot imagine it could possibly be true. It wasn't until Mike Helton came in. I figured when it was a done deal, when it was official, the bigwigs would come in. Then they did, and when they made the announcement, that's when it really set in and it was just awful – just disbelief.

At that point, you have to turn into a journalist. You have to park your feelings aside and write. We just kind of went with it. It was an incredible thing because we basically all pulled together and wrote. But I tell you, it was the first time I had a cigarette in fifteen years. I was just devastated. I just needed something to take off the edge because you can't believe this is happening. Being in the pressroom was like being at a funeral. There was just a shroud. Obviously you have people at the Daytona 500 that you won't see the rest of the year. But the core group of journalists that follow the sport week in and week out were just kind of leaning on each other to try to get us through the night. You have a job to do, and you really just have to push yourself through it.

Two weeks later when I did have that first week off – when I wasn't going to watch Vegas, I just spent two days in bed, just trying to deal with the whole situation because it was like life had gone on a free fall. If it was that bad for us on the fringe, I can't even imagine what the family must have gone through.

I think anybody who covered racing had never really got that close to him because he had been burnt so many times by opportunists trying to take advantage of his success and his immense wealth. I can

understand why he was like that. But he either trusted you or he didn't, and if he trusted you he at least accommodated you. I can remember being at Dover last year. I was doing a story on Junior and I had a question I wanted to go up and ask him and I wanted to talk about his teams. I came walking in the back of the transporter and he says, "Have a seat." He's sitting there and he has on his cheaters – his bifocals, and I'm looking at him and seeing him as a grandfather for the first time. I almost started to laugh and said, "I can't believe you're wearing your cheaters." He just looked at me like I was stupid, and I was embarrassed for saying that. But to see him in his uniform, and he has on his cheaters. He's reading Winston Cup Scene. He points to a story and says, "Hey, what do you know about this?" So he's kind of picking my brain, and I thought "okay." It was just seeing another side of him. There were certain times when you catch these people and they're not on guard and it's almost refreshing.

It might take you five or ten minutes with Dale, but you would get a quote that you would savor for months. It was just natural. He would just pop that mustache grin and you would get a tingle, 'cause you knew when he had that grin and had the smile and had the wink going, that you were going to get 'golden' Earnhardt that day. He would come up with sound bites that were just unmatched. It would like sustain you. If you're sitting there, and you're a word junkie you're just waiting for him to come up with something. When he was on, he was on, and there was just no stopping him.

It's like Junior said the other day. There are people you meet who are extremely intellectual and they've had formal education and it's great to get into the finest schools and whatever. But he had the 'school of hard knocks' and he had intuition and he had common sense that would carry him into any boardroom, into any state dinner. When he walked into the room, it was just magic, once he warmed up to you and kinda got over his shyness, because, even at fifty, he had a shyness that was refreshing.

Earnhardt and Dale Jarrett both had the trademark mustaches and when Earnhardt's was gone – apparently when he went scuba diving it interfered with his mask and he shaved it off, but it didn't take him long to grow it back out. I didn't kid him about not having the mustache because you pick your punches carefully with him. If you got on his bad side, it would take a prayer for him to get over it. The guy just didn't forget. I was sitting with a cub NASCAR reporter, an excellent investigative journalist, but he had never covered NASCAR. I watched him ask questions of Earnhardt, and Earnhardt was just shaking his head and you knew he was not going to give him the answers he was looking for.

Once I had asked Earnhardt about certain things affecting NASCAR.

Other owners had talked about franchising and perhaps getting a bigger piece of the pie. Or asking Earnhardt if NASCAR was fairly distributing the wealth among the drivers and the owners, he would just say to me, "You know better than to ask me those questions." I would just leave it at that. I wouldn't press. NASCAR helped make Dale Earnhardt, and he remembered that until the day he died. His loyalty lay with the France family. Billy, Jr. and he were quite close and Jimmy France said if it had not been for Earnhardt, he didn't think that Billy, Jr.'s cancer recovery would have gone as smoothly as it did. He said Earnhardt coming down and being part of the healing process speeded it up. That was just how he was. They had become great friends throughout the years and if you were a friend of Earnhardt's he was loyal to the end.

I know there are journalistic sides to the whole autopsy photo thing, but the fact that Teresa has persevered through it all says something about what a woman she is. He would often say she was the brains behind the business and the empire they had. For so many years before Gordon got popular, Earnhardt would outsell the entire garage. You could put the souvenir sales from everybody else in the garage together and it would not add up to what Earnhardt did in a year. That's just amazing when you think about it. It's changed quite a bit, but he's still the top dog. And I think even in his death, as long as his things are on the truck, they'll sell.

He and Teresa had a partnership between the two of them. I don't believe there is such a thing as an ideal marriage – maybe I'm just cynical. But if anyone had something that could persevere in a business as tough as racing, they had it. They complemented each other. I'd see her on the first day of school getting Taylor signed up. She combined all the talents of being a wife and a mother and a businesswoman. It's not easy to do what she's done, and she's pulled it off tremendously. She's fascinating. It's hard to get an interview with her – I wouldn't try right now because I think it would be out of bounds, but even before she just did not feel comfortable being in the public. She came from a racing family. Her father is Tommy Houston's brother, and Tommy has the two boys. His son Andy is racing Winston Cup now. Since she was already in racing when she met Earnhardt, she is greatly responsible for building their dynasty to what it is today. She was the one who made the decisions. She was the one who made the approvals of the merchandise – whether or not they thought it was up to their standards to put on the truck to sell. She's just done an incredible job. Behind every man is an incredible woman, and she fits that bill.

Will Dale Earnhardt be like Elvis? I think it already is. Just like now at DEI, it is just going to become a shrine. Junior is already saying he's having trouble going through the transition because people won't leave

him alone. But you know I think Dale Senior will be part of NASCAR legend and lore as long as the rest of us are around and just keep the stories going.

Ten years from now if somebody said describe Dale Earnhardt in just a few words, I'd say, "Probably the greatest racer ever to drive in NASCAR." I know people would dispute that because Petty had two hundred victories but that was at a time when they were racing maybe twice a week. Petty had a lot more opportunities. I know the winning percentages are extremely close but when Petty was winning, he had the best equipment available. That's not saying that R. C. didn't give Earnhardt the best. Had they had their act together in the mid-nineties, I'm not sure what went wrong in the transition, but had they not kind of missed a step, I think Earnhardt would have had that eighth championship and probably it would not have been a problem getting up to 90 – 100 victories. I think he will probably go down as the greatest NASCAR driver of all times. The dynasty he left behind, depending on if DEI stays on the course it's on now; they will be a championship organization.

I would say that Earnhardt did the most coming from nothing. The one thing that female journalists have going for them, at least when they get to be my age and have a couple of kids, is they look at life a little bit differently. Racing is not the 'end all.' These people have families. They are mothers, fathers, they have sons and daughters. I think if you can relate to them at that level you see them in a different light than just a guy who's out there driving the race car. And once you get below the surface, I think it opens itself to better understanding these people and to the story itself.

Growing up in St. Louis, the Sporting News was just the baseball bible. If you're a big baseball fan, you were dialed into what the Sporting News had to say because they were on the cutting edge of anything that was baseball. I kind of lost touch with it over the years and so one of my editors took a job there doing their on-line for Motor Sports and getting back into the magazine side of it and having the opportunity to launch the NASCAR pages this year has been a rewarding opportunity for all of us because it has given people who may not have been exposed to NASCAR an inside look at how the sport has grown to the point it has – to the point where The Sporting News has taken an interest in putting it in the magazine. It says something for NASCAR and it says something for The Sporting News, and I just hope it's a healthy marriage that continues.

For the last three years, I've been contributing to the Motor Sports website. Then a year ago, I did a Joe Gibbs story right around Super Bowl time and they figured it would be neat just to do a "Here's Joe Gibbs, two-time Super Bowl champion coach, but now he's racing." Just kind of test the waters and see if people would go for it, and a year later we were putting it in as the seventh sport in the magazine so it must have caught somebody's eye.

Earnhardt had a small group of friends. I don't want it to seem like I was in that inner circle, but he showed me such graciousness. Everybody said that Earnhardt liked women, but I think he respected women. I think that's why he acted this way. Some of these guys can't be bothered with you, but he had a respect for women that wasn't like some of these guys – not that horn dog kind of stuff – just respect. I don't think there's going to be another one like him and that's the hardest thing to deal with. That was the classy side of him. Like I said, the coolest thing about our relationship is I got to see him be a dad in addition to just being a driver. Uncovering those layers was just more rewarding at times than watching him in the race car.

The first time I interviewed Dale, Jr., and this was before he made his Busch debut at Myrtle Beach, was five-six years ago, this was just a kid who never really felt he had his father's attention. He knew if he wanted his father's attention, he had to go out there and prove himself on the track. That was the only way. He did that. If you saw the interview with Junior on Fox, he knew that he had accomplished what he set out to do – which was make his dad happy, and he did that.

My husband Reid covered Earnhardt when he was dirt racing with his dad at Metrolina. That was earlier when Reid graduated from Yale and went to work at the Charlotte Observer; he would run around with Tom Higgins and would cover the dirt track races. He and David Green, when David was putting together the pictorial that they did for Auto World Weekly, he was calling Reid and they were going through the history books and just going through their minds and pulling up stories.

Dale Earnhardt was a neat guy.

(At this point, Reid Spencer, Lee's husband joined the conversation. Reid played #1 on the Yale Golf team for four years. After an extensive period of covering auto racing for the Charlotte Observer, he now owns Metrolina Golf, a publication covering that sport in the Carolinas.)

As Benny Parsons said, way back when, he didn't think Earnhardt had the wherewithal to represent a major company with polish, and Benny classily admitted that he was wrong. Earnhardt merchandise was second to none and so I think if you would ask people about that end of the business, they would have said, "No way." Back in those days, he was basically a country guy from a mill town and not the sort of 'slick corporate representative' that you would think it would take to make that kind of money. It was nothing like Jeff Gordon when Jeff Gordon arrived on the scene as an almost ready-made spokesperson.

The day Dale passed, I was home watching the race on television. Lee was in the infield at Daytona. It looked like one of those crashes which on the surface doesn't appear that bad but you sort of had a sense that it might be. Then when I saw the interview with Kenny Schrader after he had looked in Earnhardt's window, and Kenny looked as if he had gone three shades of gray. So at that point, you sort of knew something was really wrong. He was clearly shaken up. The irony of the whole thing for me – the broadcast did not really concentrate on what might be wrong with Earnhardt. Because it was Darrell Waltrip in the booth and Michael in Victory Lane, they really concentrated on Michael's winning the race. I don't think you can really blame them for that, but I thought they were remiss in not following up and finding out about Earnhardt because that was the question on everybody's mind as the race ended. What happened to Earnhardt? You know that when Earnhardt does not lower the window netting and get out of the car, it's because he is physically unable to do so.

We live about twenty miles north of Charlotte, near Davidson. I cover the minor league baseball team over there which happens to be the Kannapolis Intimidators, renamed this year because Earnhardt bought a small interest in the team back in November, along with Bruton Smith. I think his buying into the team was an altruistic thing on his part because the team had been struggling, both with acceptance in the community and with attendance. I think he was willing to lend his name to the team to try to make them more successful. I think it would have worked – and may still. They have decided to keep the name. DEI and the Earnhardt family still support the effort so I think it may well help.

What happened at the DEI was pretty amazing with all the flowers, memorabilia, and all the things the fans brought up there during the subsequent week.

All of that is an incredible tribute to Dale Earnhardt.

Mike Went To A Really Tough Hebrew School. They Had Nuns.

Mike Harris

*For all the thousands of stories written about Dale Earnhardt
after his passing, one of the very best was by long-time
Associated Press writer, Mike Harris. Harris, in the article,
wrote about special memories he shared with Dale.*

It was the first and only first-person column I've ever done at AP in
thirty-two years. I've never written a story before with the word "I" in
it that wasn't in a quote. The reason I did this was because I went to
the memorial service and was very disappointed in it. I don't come from
the south but from what I'm told, this was a very traditional Southern
Baptist service. It was very religiously oriented, very little personal stuff
and the family didn't even talk. There were no stories. I'm from a different tradition. I'm a Jew, and I'm from a tradition where we said "Sheva"
in seven days and we go to a relative's home for seven days after a death.
That's the traditional way, but not everyone does it for that long anymore
– maybe just one day or so. But you go and you have a lot of food and you
tell stories. It's like an Irish wake, without the drinking. We drink when
we eat, and they drink! We sit and talk and tell stories about the person,
and we relate to each other and it makes you feel better and it helps you
get past your grief. I didn't find this to be very helpful to me at all in getting over the death of this man who I didn't necessarily consider a friend
but a very good acquaintance.

I knew him for twenty-one years, and you spend a lot of moments
over the years together, and even if you're not good friends, you feel a connection. I was telling this to my boss that it wasn't very satisfying, and I
could have gotten up there and told twenty minutes of stories. She said,
"Well, do it." I said, "What do you mean?" She said, "Write it, tell some stories." I said, "Well, I've never done that." She said, "Do it now." She said,
"Write it, and see how you feel about it. If you want to use it, we'll use it."

I got a very positive response. Normally I don't get any response
from the fans – from readers. They don't know how to reach us, and AP
people are pretty anonymous. But I got notes from about a half dozen of

my colleagues, which doesn't usually happen, just saying, "Really enjoyed reading that. Nice job." That kind of thing.

Just a couple of days before he died, I was at an IROC luncheon, and I was sitting with him at the table. Bobby Allison and his wife Judy were also sitting at the table. They were telling stories and having a good time. They hadn't seen each other for a while. There's a woman by the name of Barbara Signore who is the wife of the IROC Series President, and Barbara has a little trouble walking. She was up on the stage, maybe two feet in the air, and they were giving her an award for all the years they had been involved in the sport – I think it was the 25th anniversary or whatever. Anyway Dale was so concerned when she was leaving the stage because he was afraid she was going to trip and fall off the stage. He was sitting right near the front. He said, "Hey, somebody help her." He started to get up, but somebody else moved over to help Barb. Nobody else made that kind of reaction. He was the one who noticed and made sure somebody took care of Barb to step down.

The other thing that happened the same day, just a couple of minutes later, was there was a "Make-a-Wish" child there who presented him with a framed picture of some kind which the boy had drawn. He called all the other IROC drivers up and said, "You guys get up here and take a picture with this kid." He lined everybody up and made sure the picture was taken with all the IROC drivers.

That's the kind of guy he was. He didn't like to show it to the public but it was really there. He was a good man in a lot of ways. He was sometimes very difficult to deal with. There was a period of about a year and a half when we didn't even speak except in mass interviews. He was angry at something I had written. Then one day, it must have been about a year and a half later, I was in Talladega, and I'm walking through the garage area. I see him walking the other way, and I just nodded at him as I'm walking past. I was walking slow, kind of looking around, and all of a sudden, I feel this poke in my ribs. I looked around, and he has this big grin on his face and said, "Don't you say hello anymore?" That was the end of that. I still to this day don't know why I was persona non grata any more. We were fine after that.

He was a little bit strange at times. He was sometimes very difficult to read. I came to like him very much. I really heard so many good things about him. I always had good luck with him as far as stories were concerned. Unless he was really busy or distracted, he was a wonderful interview. If you had his attention, he gave you book and verse about things and did it in such a way that it was interesting and positive. I enjoyed dealing with him very much. I wouldn't consider us friends, but we were certainly good acquaintances.

His daughter was the first Earnhardt to graduate from college and he was very proud of her. I think he was amazed that she had done that because nobody else in their family had ever gone that far in school. Whenever he would talk about it, you could see how proud he was and how filled with amazement he was over the whole thing. She's a pretty sharp kid. I'm not for sure, but I think she went to UNC-Charlotte.

At Talladega last year, Dale was so far back that it was never in my thoughts that he could come to the front and win. The one thought I had, with about twenty laps to go, when I saw him fading in the pack was, "Well, that's too bad." And I kind of forgot about him, until all of a sudden there he was back up front again. I couldn't believe it. It was awesome. I believe that may have been his greatest race.

Courtesy of IMHF

Kerry, Kelley, Dale Jr.

Monte Was Flabbergasted, And It Has Been A Long Time Since Monte's Flabber Had Been Gasted.

Monte Dutton

Monte Dutton writes like Dale Earnhardt raced: hard, fast and forward. Dutton's place is the Gaston Gazette in Gastonia, N. C. He heads up their auto racing coverage and edits NASCAR This Week, a syndicated page that is the most widely-read NASCAR news each week. His new book with Tony Stewart, "Rebel With a Cause" came out in early summer, 2000.

I think this is my ninth year covering racing pretty regularly. Of course I've been around Dale Earnhardt a lot in that amount of time. Earnhardt was a guy they called The Intimidator, and he was intimidating to interview. I think it was one of those things where you sort of had to stand up to him to do an interview. And I guess I learned that. A typical interview with Earnhardt would have involved you asking a question and then he sort of fires back, "What the h— do you mean by that?" And then you say, "Well I mean, damn it, this..." And then he would give you a good answer, and he would give you that sort of little mischievous grin of his. It was just one of those things where you sort of had to have a little argument with him first, and then you get your interview.

One of the things I remember is if he didn't want to talk to the media, it didn't matter, he wasn't going to. If he did, he'd sort of summoned you. Last fall at Richmond, he was upset about the impending use of restrictor plates for a race at New Hampshire. He got really irritated about that. I got to the track and walked down to the infield media center around 8:00 in the morning. I still had a backpack on. I got a tap on the shoulder and was told, "Earnhardt wants to see you in his trailer in fifteen minutes." My first thought was, "What the heck is he mad at me for now?" I was like – "I just saw him yesterday."

There had been this promotional thing that Winston had put on at Langley Air Force Base. He had been there, and I had chatted with him and kidded around. It didn't occur to me what he would actually want – basically what he wanted was to propagandize. He was angry about the impending rules change and he wanted to air his grievances. He probably chose me because he knew that I kind of have a 'pull-no-punches' attitude so he thought I'd raise as much h_ll as anybody. He wanted somebody who was really going to use his ammunition and criticize them. So I went over there and what followed was probably the best hour I've spent covering NASCAR. He held court on a wide range of topics. He was often very profane. He made a lot of disparaging remarks. At one point when he was talking, everybody had a tape, and there were maybe three sports writers there. Everyone had tape recorders but as a general rule, I'll have a note pad and will be jotting down a few things sort of as a guide so if it's something I'm not interested in, I won't have to transcribe the whole thing. It sort of prompts me to look for certain items. He was saying something that was particularly inflammatory and he looked up and I was scribbling and he said, "Don't be writing that s_ _t down." At the same time, he winged an empty bottle of Powerade or Gatorade and hit me right in the wrist where I was writing. I just looked up at him and said, "I take that as off the record, huh?" He started laughing.

When the thing was over, we walked out of the lounge area of Richard Childress' transporter and he said something like, "All right guys, thanks for coming. Don't kill me too bad in the paper." When he said that, I whirled around and said, "You knew exactly what you were doing when you invited us over here." He got that grin again, and laughed at that.

I have to say I didn't hang out with Earnhardt that much. He's a guy, to be honest, for a good bit of the time I've covered races, I've always respected but didn't particularly like. He can be a very difficult man to deal with. Last year I think is the only year that I've ever had covering races that Earnhardt and I didn't have any major falling out. I guess part of it may be that he got used to me, and I got used to him. I don't know.

There have been a lot of times when he has made things very difficult for me. I once wrote a column about spending a whole weekend unsuccessfully trying to talk with him. At one point, I was waiting outside to talk with him and while his publicist held people at bay, he scooted out the side door. I saw it, and I sort of chased him. We went a little ways with me asking questions and him not replying to them. So I actually wrote a humorous column about the whole weekend of "How Earnhardt didn't talk to anybody."

I'll tell you what I think. Earnhardt is Earnhardt, a guy who came from humble roots. Even though he's the son of a race car driver he was not the son of a race car driver who amassed a great deal of wealth. I think that before now, most race car drivers were like that. Nowadays, the sport has gotten so expensive that you don't have these guys rise up from the dirt tracks with nothing but the clothes on their backs. So I think that one of the things about Earnhardt, I think he had a certain chip on his shoulder. I also think this is one of the things that made people love him. For every guy who has a blue collar job and struggles to make a living, I think their feeling is that first of all he never stopped being one of them no matter how much wealth he got. Secondly, I think they felt that "but for the grace of God, if I had the ability he had, I could be Dale Earnhardt." So I think sometimes one of the things about Earnhardt that made him so contrary was because of the fact he had probably come along poor, having a lot of times when he didn't know how he was going to pay for the car, pay for the equipment he was buying, I think when he got prominent and made it, I think he sort of took pride in having so much that he could do whatever he wanted to. Like, "I don't care if everybody wants to talk to me, if I don't want to talk, I don't have to." And I think what you had to do is you had to learn that he had that attitude. Sometimes by confronting him and throwing it in his face, you could get him to talk to you when maybe he wouldn't talk to anyone else.

I guess these are not warm and fuzzy stories, but he was not a warm and fuzzy man. He was a guy who has my sort of grudging respect. Actually the darndest thing was, the last three or four weeks before he died, there are several incidents that happened that struck me as being quite abnormal for Earnhardt. I was in Daytona for the whole month. I watched him run the Rolex 24 and after he had a driving stint in the sports car, he had a little makeshift interview session and was very cooperative. He actually came driving over in a golf cart, and we were waiting for him in an abandoned building. He sat there and answered all the questions. After the last question I asked, "I said, okay, thanks, I appreciate it." He looked at me, and he put his fist out. What he wanted me to do is hit my fist on top of his. This was an extremely unlikely, unusual thing for him to do to a press guy.

The other thing is, as a journalist, we don't often show that sort of fan interest. So I felt really awkward, as I stuck my hand out, he boxed my wrist on top of his. First of all, I felt sheepish because it's not the type thing you want to do. It was like high-fiving with a guy. Secondly, it caught me completely by surprise. It was just really unlike him.

A couple of days later, I was at a function where he was. He happened to come along in the dinner line. I started talking with him. He started telling me how he'd like to race in the Sweetbriar again next year and started chatting with me very pleasantly. He was standing there, and he took a roll and instead of putting it on his plate, he put it on mine. That also left me flabbergasted. We'd had sort of an adversarial relationship over the years. And that was not just with me but with many of the people in the media. There are times as a journalist when your boss says he wants a story on Earnhardt. They won't take no for an answer. Sometimes Earnhardt would just not talk to you. He was a guy who would do it damn well the way he wanted to. He was in an uncommonly pleasant mood the last few weeks of his life.

The same time that I was at that function he went over and started chatting to a kid in a wheelchair, like sometimes you see kids from the Make-A-Wish Foundation. This was at the International Race of Champions, and they were drawing starting positions for the race at Daytona, Dale Earnhardt sort of boisterously got up and commanded all the other drivers to come up and have a picture taken with this kid. They immediately, when he said something, just jumped. Those same guys who might have been slipping out the back door to get back to the track, the minute Earnhardt said, "Come up here, we're going to take a picture." They all went up and took a picture. He was a guy who could be that way, but I saw the people around him. There were a lot of times during his career that he completely ignored autograph seekers and such. He would just walk right through them like they didn't exist. Then there were other times, when he would go out and sign autographs for half an hour. For people who knew him, they always expressed that they could never anticipate when the guy who signed the autographs was going to show up – you couldn't drag him with twelve white horses to do that unless he wanted to do that.

On occasion there might be fifty fans show up wanting to get his autograph or picture. When he was mad at NASCAR about something, what he would do is – he would walk out of his trailer, walk over there to the NASCAR trailer, stand outside, knowing full well that a huge crowd would develop and no one could get a damn thing done over there. And he would do that for spite. He would do that if he was mad. I've known of him doing that more than one time.

We have a syndicated page at the Gaston Gazette where I work, and I've said, "What is it about the loss of a well-known figure that makes everybody think they are like a poet or a song writer?" I must have read fifty horrible poems. Some even came in the mail to me. Imagine how many were mailed to his race shop. Most were just horrible – like: "I love you Dale, you hit the wall, and that ain't all, a part of me." – just awful, awful, awful poetry. People leave these tributes to this icon. I really thought most of the ones I saw were awful, which makes me a terrible snob, I might add.

I've refused to run any of them. I've already gotten return letters from people mad that we haven't done it. First of all, we don't have the

car driver from the time he's driving some beat-up Pinto at the local dirt track, the expenses are such that he has to have a sponsor and he has an obligation to that. Actually one time in a column, I wrote, 'Because auto racing is inherently commercial, all the drivers won't talk to you. Because auto racing is so inherently commercial, none of them will say a damn thing.' Earnhardt was a guy that you got him, and he didn't give a damn. I think one of the key things with Earnhardt was coming up with a sponsor who'd let him be himself. Earnhardt wasn't going to kowtow to anybody. I can tell you right now that people from Chevrolet won't talk about it on the record now that he's gone, but there's many times where just because they wanted him to do something, it's didn't matter. If he didn't want to do it, he wasn't going to do it. He was so good, and he was so big, and he had so many fans that they had to put up with it. This is a very, very independent person. I think sometimes he was contrary just to be contrary 'cause he got a kick out of it.

Earnhardt, whether you liked him or disliked him, you might have said he was selfish as a race car driver and wouldn't work with anybody, but you knew that going in. I think that with many of the other drivers, first of all they respect him because he was so damn good. Secondly, in racing, if somebody does something, and you don't like it, do something about it. Earnhardt was so good they couldn't do anything about it so they had to go along with it. He really was an indomitable figure of legendary renown. There's going to be stories about him in which people tell you things he did that they've never seen anybody do.

He really was a guy who cheated death for a long time. I think the first reaction when he was killed was that it couldn't possibly happen to Dale Earnhardt. He seemed immortal in a race car. I've actually had people write me letters about how they can't conceive of him making what seemed to be the mistake that killed him. My view of what happened in the wreck is that I think his car started to get wobbly and I think the unfortunate thing was that right at the moment that he was correcting, he got tapped from behind.

There's no blame there because in racing when a car is going bumper to bumper with another car at 200 miles per hour, people always blame it on the guy who is behind but usually it's the guy in front letting up just a little bit. Earnhardt had to lift a little bit because his car was a little out of control. When he lifted, just at the moment he was probably straightening the car out, he got tapped from behind. That's probably the moment when he was turning the wheel back to the right to correct it. But when he got that little bump from behind, that turned a small correction into a wild over-correction. That's why he went into the wall so hard. But it's still mysterious, 'cause most people who saw the crash can't imagine it. I've had people write me and they think that for Earnhardt to have crashed like that, he must have had something like a heart attack or something. They can't imagine him making a mistake that took his own life. I actually wrote a person back the very thing I just told you. I think that he just turned the car a little bit to the right and got the tap from behind which probably caused the car to turn radically harder to the right. That's the way most tragedies are – whether they are in the twinkling of an instant or a comedy of errors. Whether it's just some guy who broke up with his girl-friend, and that put him in a dark mood. He started drinking then he ran into somebody and the next thing you know, the guy's killed in a car wreck. There was a small, tiny comedy of errors that took Dale Earnhardt to his fate. This took place over a period of a couple of seconds. But even there, a guy's been cheating fate all the time, the odds all of a sudden caught up with him in that awful fateful moment.

NASCAR has always had a lot of control over things like that. It's an obstacle to the sport's growth because the people want to hear it like it is. You're not going to get the ratings that you would have otherwise if you don't build it.

I could have written an official book on Tony Stewart, but refused. He said, "Why?" I said, "Because it will suck." And Tony was good with that. Now when the book is out, he may not speak to me again 'cause you never can tell, but I think he will because he's that good a guy. And I think he understands that. I said, "Tony, it's like this. If you want to tell me something off the record, fine. But you've got to make sure it's off the record because I can keep a secret. If you tell me not to tell anybody, I won't tell my mother. But if you don't tell me not to tell anybody, I'll tell the whole world 'cause that's my job." One time Tony Stewart told me he was going to run in a midget car race somewhere so I put it in that day's paper – that he was going to run in a midget car race. Next time he saw me he said, "Oh man, you got me in all kinds of trouble." I said, "Well you told me that," and he said he just thought I would be interested in it. I said, "Tony, how many times have we got to go over this?" You said you'd be interested in this. "I took that as a scoop for my buddy, Monte." He took it to mean we were just talking as friends. Well, I'll talk to him as a friend, but you've got to be sure we're clear on that.

I'm assuming that the book you're writing is not official. I know that Leigh Montville is writing a book and has supposedly gotten two hundred thousand, and it's an official book. Anything that's interesting, someone will take out of it. I won't write official books anyway because in general people have a tendency to – "Oh, this rubs me the wrong way." By the time the sponsor and NASCAR and Chevrolet and all these people quit excising things you wrote, there's not anything left. I would just write a novel loosely based on Earnhardt; not really be Earnhardt, just have Earnhardt in mind when I write it. Matter of fact, I've written two chapters of something like that. If I had the time, I'd want to get a proposal.

I wrote a book last year called "At Speed," a collection of columns. I'm going to have another book on driver, Tony Stewart, which will be out in about a month. But my agent doesn't handle fiction 'cause he never can make any money off of it. So I'm going to have to do this from square one, so I probably will never do it. I would like to write a stock car racing novel that is just completely telling all – no holds barred. And I would like for the character of Earnhardt – I mean not be Earnhardt or based on the events of his life, but just have him in mind when I'm writing it. You cannot be hypocritical about Earnhardt, because he was a guy I didn't have a great deal of love for, but I had a lot of respect for. It really bothers me how a lot of people that wouldn't give the guy the time of day all of a sudden are his best friends.

As to the autopsy photos, it's very simple. They're not designed for a race car driver who was killed. They're designed where if the president were assassinated and people doubted the official version. They're designed so an independent person who's not there can make sure that the powers that be are acting properly. I decry as much as anybody somebody who would run autopsy pictures on their web site. But some guy wrote me the other day and said that some web site now has gotten pictures from the death of Neil Bonnett in 1994. I wrote the guy back and said, "You're doing exactly what this guy did, when you pulled it up and found them there and looked at them." That's exactly what he put them there for – for hits on his web site so he could charge more for advertising. And by calling that thing up, you did exactly what he wanted you to do.

The Orlando Sentinel wasn't going to do that. All they wanted to do was have an independent observer look at them to make sure that what has been cited as the cause of death was correct. Because there are a lot of areas where you just can't trust NASCAR. NASCAR is very concerned about liability issues and things like that. Most of us don't believe that Earnhardt's seatbelt broke. We believe that's the course of least resistance. What's wrong is those cars are too rigid in the front and they don't give and the body takes all the shock. And NASCAR rather than having to change the way cars are built, which they might quietly do over time, would rather palm it off on something else so that's what the Orlando Sentinel wanted those pictures for.

Earnhardt Was Just A Regular Guy Who Sometimes Wore A Cape.

Deb Williams

Deb Williams, outstanding reporter for the Winston Cup Scene, and Dale Earnhardt both grew up in mill towns and as a result developed a mutual respect and understanding. Williams watched him progress from the days when he had to take out thirty-day notes to pay for needed parts.

D ale Earnhardt's rookie season, 1979, was my first year with UPI and that's when I started covering Winston Cup racing. I was already familiar with the Earnhardt family because in the late 50s and early 60s his father, Ralph, had driven for family friends, Frank and Hilda Presley in Canton, North Carolina.

Covering him was interesting but also frustrating at times because of his personality. You knew immediately if he liked you or didn't like you. If he did, he would tease you. The frustrating part would be if you were on deadline and had to talk to him when he was busy. I don't think a lot of people understood what a good heart he had. In talking with his mother, I could see the closeness the family had. His growing up years weren't all peaches and cream; it was tough. Back when Ralph was racing, the money wasn't there like it is today, and racing was not viewed as something the pillars of the community did.

It was looked down on by other people – that's just a rough and rowdy crowd! They had a large family and I can't remember that Martha worked outside the home, by today's standards, they didn't have a lot of material things. They never went hungry. They had plenty of clothes and food to eat. They had what mattered which was the family and the love of the family.

The things I could see in him were his heart and his desire. When anybody is willing to take out thirty-day notes and sixty-day notes and ninety-day notes and pay them off with what they won, when they lay on a crawler underneath a car, and they fall asleep with a wrench in their hand while working on their car and wake up and go right back to working on the car – that's what sets him apart from others – he's a racer, his heart and his desire. He was also fortunate that his body didn't require a lot of sleep.

He was one of those who can do power naps, but you're not going to find many people who would get up at four in the morning, go into the office and sign autographs until eight o'clock. He had the desire and the determination, the hard-headedness, if you like. His dad was nicknamed 'Ironheart.' Dale was nicknamed 'Ironhead.' His nicknames were 'Ironhead,' 'The Intimidator,' and of course 'The Man in Black.' Before 'The Intimidator' came along, it was 'Ironhead.'

Teresa had a real estate license. She was the one who set up the dealership when they got in the management team, called Dale in when they needed his signature. As he became more prominent and his image became so marketable, she is the one who approved every single photo that went out of there. "Yes, this was right; no, this was wrong." – that type of thing. When we (Street and Smith) did a tour book for them a year or so ago to sell on the souvenir rig, every photo that went in was approved by Teresa. If Dale didn't have any problem with the photo, but Teresa didn't like it, it wasn't used. They had a very special relationship. He had the racing savvy and, of course, one thing that helped tremendously was her being from a racing family. She grew up in racing just like he did. Teresa's maiden name is Houston, and Tommy Houston, who drove in the Busch series, is her uncle. Andy Houston, who drives the '96' car is her first cousin. In fact where she and Dale met was at Hickory Motor Speedway. She was about ten years younger than Dale. When Dale was racing at Hickory long before he ever went Winston Cup, she was around there, too.

As I began covering Dale, when he began to win the championships, I was initially very tentative. Lots of times I would let the other people ask the questions. I was used to Richard Petty's personality, and the fact that Earnhardt was not that open was one of those situations where I felt I needed to observe and figure out the best way to handle the situation. As I was around him more and learned him more and became more familiar with Teresa, I felt more comfortable just to go up and talk with him. I think he felt more comfortable with me on the same level. One thing that really helped was that one time in Talladega, this would have been in the nineties, I came out of the media center and was leaving for the day. Teresa was sitting over by the motor home, and Taylor was riding her bicycle. I just went over and started talking to Teresa. We were sitting there talking when Dale came out. The three of us just sat there and talked while Taylor rode her bicycle like we were sitting out in the front yard somewhere talking.

When you had Dale Earnhardt's trust, it meant everything. You knew he wasn't going to BS you. You knew he was going to give time for you when he could. There was mutual trust and respect between you, because with him there had to be trust and respect.

I feel like we had a lot of things in common because both of us grew up in mill towns. He grew up in a textile mill town. I grew up in a paper mill town, Canton, North Carolina

When I started seeing the video replays of the accident that Monday and Tuesday, something was wrong with them. I couldn't figure out what I had seen when I watching it all happen that I wasn't seeing on the video tapes. Then it dawned on me and I realized what it was when I was sitting in the memorial service that Thursday. It was how bright everything was. How beautiful everything was. The bright light that I saw as they came through turn four was not being picked up on the video. It was about four thirty in the afternoon when it happened but I remembered it had been as bright like it was noon or one o'clock.

To me, it doesn't seem real. You thought of him as being invincible. It would happen to everybody else, not him. I've known Adam Petty since he was a baby, and I still catch myself looking for his name in the Busch series lineup. With Dale, it seems like, "Okay, he's hurt, he's away, he's recuperating, but he'll be back." When we were putting our special section together to pay tribute to him, I didn't feel like we were putting together a memorial section, I felt like we were putting together the section we would have put together for his last year had he retired.

A motor sports writer from Cleveland told me she tried to explain things to a columnist USA Today had sent down there who had never been to a race before. The columnist from USA Today asked her when it happened, "Is this big?" The Cleveland motor sports writer looked at her and said, "Let me explain it to you. This is the same as the final game of NBA playoffs with Michael Jordan driving the lane to the basket to make the winning shot and he has a heart attack before he gets there and dies – that's how big this is." When she put it to that columnist in that manner, the columnist understood.

Chapter 7

Donald J. Mahoney

Kelly Collins

Dan Hughes

Eli Gold

Chet Coppock

Steve Byrnes

Mike Lee

Bob Latford

Dick Berggren

The White Flag

Men Love Sports Illustrated. They Prove It Every February With That One Issue.

Donald J. Mahoney

Director, Special Publications, Sports Illustrated

We covet the Sports Illustrated cover, as a time-honored tradition and a lot of history is attached to being on the cover. We're very selective about topics we do but here was clearly a gentleman deserving a commemorative. That's a side of our business we reserve for celebratory situations. Annually we do Super Bowl, Final Four, Oklahoma winning the national title. We do the NHL Stanley Cup and the NBA Championship and, of course, the World Series. Then as situations arise where people retiring or, God forbid, in the case of Dale, passing away, we honor them with an editorial piece. The same kind of care and concern that goes into the weekly issue goes into that.

This was the most issues we've ever printed of a commemorative. It sold out, and at the request of wholesalers, distributors and fans, we went back to the printers for more. The distribution and sale of that piece is now legend. We first printed one million copies, then went back to press for 550,000. We never expected it to sell like that.

We realized the extent of Earnhardt's passing right away. There are heroes in every sport. We cover NASCAR as part of the regular realm of sports coverage that we do here at Sports Illustrated, including a bunch of special sections a year that we do on NASCAR and other segments of auto racing. Certainly Dale was somebody who had charismatic charm that obviously attracted the following he had. Speculation was rampant that the fans would be clamoring for memorabilia and the histrionics of his career, and we felt we'd be in the best position to document that history and celebrate his life. Our distribution of the commemorative issue was lower two thirds of the nation with sporadic northern exposure.

I hate to have to look at a project like this because it's not really what we were all about. There was a lot said about it in understanding that his wife did not want advertisers, sponsors and what not to support something like this. But this was needed; it was a healing process for fans. Truthfully it shocked me, that within my circle of friends, the number of people who were Dale Earnhardt fans. I love the sport of auto racing. NASCAR is not at the top of my list. I prefer track racing. The number of people that I know who are passionate about NASCAR shocked me, and particularly how upset they got over this tragedy.

Always, the managing editor of Sports Illustrated is who makes the call on doing special issues. He judges it based on the appropriateness of that individual being deserving of a cover of SI, and then the issues surrounding the reason for it with a great deal of sensitivity to the fact that in this particular case, as with a number of others involving someone passing, we don't take that lightly. We don't, by any means, want to give the impression that this was strictly focused on a business decision because it definitely was not. The decision was made to put a top-quality product out that next weekend or early in the following week. There were other people out there with product within forty-eight hours, but we don't do it that way. We take the time to do it right. If the name Sports Illustrated is going to be on it, we want it to be representative of everything we do.

In running this division for four years, I've never had such a great number of phone calls from fans on two fronts. One was congratulations on an outstanding piece, "It's the best one I've seen," from some pretty influential people. And we've never had so many people call asking where they could get this copy, particularly in the northern part of the country where it wasn't as widely distributed. We had to tell them to call relatives in the south. One Kmart blew out twenty thousand copies in a week. We had stories of people coming in and buying armfuls of them to give to relatives and friends. I, too, think of the probably fifty special issues that were done in my tenure that it was the best effort that we did. I was really happy about it, given the circumstances around it. We have experts in this business to determine the number of copies to print. They get a pretty good pulse from the marketplace based on the interest of wholesalers. The biggest issue, in a situation like this, is having enough copies to meet the appetite and not getting people angry with you if it's unavailable. Our decision to reprint was made in a matter of days. We have gone back on press to reprint some regular weekly issues for additional newsstand distribution and done some interesting things with covers on the local market basis. We've been in this business since 1993 when Alabama won the national championship and a wholesaler in Alabama came to us and said, "You didn't put them on the cover, and everybody down here is furious." It was a time at which we had a year-end double issue, so we were out of the market for a week. The next issue finally came on board ten days after they'd won the national championship. So we had covered it in the magazine, but we had Dick Butkus on the cover, for whatever reason. We had to go back on-press with that one. We do a NASCAR commemorative every year – a year-end recap of the entire season that's 'newsstand only' and half a million copies.

The Goodwrench ad on the back cover was one of the number of advertisers who took the time – given the short window of opportunity – to create Earnhardt-specific creative ads. But a number of additional advertisers, because of his wife's wishes, pulled out and chose not to do it because of her request. There were four or five ads that ran in the issue that were directed at Dale.

Managing Editor, Bill Colson pulls the trigger. As soon as we heard of his death, we had a sense of Earnhardt's presence, and we had a sense of their constituency's appetite for this, and the appropriateness of an individual with his accomplishments being on the cover. It mentally comes together, and it passes muster with ones making the decision, with Colson being the final point of decision. That was a holiday weekend and the editors work different weekends. I called David Bauer, and we met early on Tuesday and took it to Colson probably Tuesday afternoon, and I think he approved it right on the spot or a little later the same day. My responsibility is more related to the sale of advertising and the distribution side of the product. David Bauer, the Editorial side, is the one who put the masterpiece together. I can take no credit, nor should I, for the outstanding job he did. If you look at all the commemoratives he does, you know that he and his team, SI Presents, are all first-class Sports Illustrated editorial talent, particularly with a commemorative of this magnitude and scope, given again the sensitivity of the issue involving his passing. They create a timetable for production to live by. Production and distribution people, for very obvious business reasons, would probably like to have the time table expedited, but David and editorial which controls this magazine, because of the church and state situation here – church being editorial versus business being the state, set a time table within comfort level to get this thing done in an expeditious manner, but making sure they don't look at it after it's done and say, "We rushed this. We should have taken more time and gotten it right."

Race Car Spelled Backward Is Race Car

Kelly Collins

Kelly Collins is a renowned Sports Car racer with great success in the 24 Hours of Le Mans, 12 Hours of Sebring and the Rolex 24 Hours at Daytona. Even with his vast experience in the IMSA, Grand Am, and ALMS series he considers the 2001 Rolex 24 Hours at Daytona the highlight of his career. Why? His co-drivers along with Andy Pilgrim were Dale Jr. and Dale Sr., all driving for the factory Corvette team.

General Motors put this program together, and I didn't even know Dale until we started testing. Andy, my teammate, and I became good friends with Dale, and we all did a lot of personal things together. Who would ever have thought he was going to die? It's funny how there are so many people who have questions and want information. They all ask how it came about or what you guys did together, or were you friends, or this and that. I've been pretty well bombarded and I've pretty much stayed to myself about the whole thing because I figure a lot of that stuff is my own personal experiences that I had with a guy. It was kinda like hanging with Elvis. He was larger than life when he was alive. The last time he stood on a podium was with his son and Andy and me. I want to be respectful to the family. They've been bombarded, too. They told Connie Chung to 'get lost.' You know how many stories really could be printed about Dale Earnhardt 'cause he was such a flamboyant character, and everything he did, and he was so strong, his persona and his being, that there's a million stories from everybody.

I only knew the man four months. What a cool guy he was. Dale had never driven that type of sports car and quite honestly I was supposed to be in the other car with Ron Fellows. They did not know where to put me. They knew they were going to need me on that car, but they didn't want to. When it was suggested to Dale, Dale was like, "Well if we normally do it with three drivers, there's no reason we can't do it with Andy and my son and myself. He didn't need any outside help. But when he realized what it took to drive one of those cars, the physical part of it and the fact that it was at night and that it could rain, Andy and Doug, our boss, kept on saying, "Kelly is normally in this car." When he met me, we hit it off, and talked and he said, "You're the same size as me and my kid, do you want to drive my car?" I said, "It's not my decision." It just went from there. We established a kind of rapport. We were jokesters with one another.

I think Dale loved the whole experience. He and Andy became good friends. It brought him closer to his son. It gave him the opportunity to be friends and allies with other race car drivers. This was a whole different kind of race. Except for the race car, it's totally different. The amount of braking, up shifting, downshifting, around the clock through rain, you turn right as well as left, you have to deal with passing slower cars but then faster cars are passing you. You have to stay out of trouble and save your tires. In NASCAR, the car is fine-tuned, and the race is long, but the physical demands come from the heat in the car and the G-loads. This comes more from shifting and braking and clutching and steering in both directions. You have to look in your rear-view mirror half the time, while NASCAR drivers don't.

I have a feeling it would be very different for me to try to just step in and compete in NASCAR. But competing is competing, and I think I probably could do okay with the right equipment.

A good NASCAR driver probably wouldn't do as well as Dale if he just jumped in a 24-hour race tomorrow. You have to remember Dale Earnhardt is Dale Earnhardt. Ninth grade was as far as he went in school, but he was the equivalent of the John Waynes of the world. He got to where he was by driving, not by self-promotion. For many years, and still to this day, a lot of people didn't like him but respected him because of how he was. First and foremost, he was a driving force. He's a natural at driving. He can finesse cars. He has a good feel and that's why he is who he is. He established himself by race wins.

I wasn't surprised at how well Dale Jr. did. I just felt he has to do good based on the will and the pressure of being an Earnhardt. He's fearless. Leave the fear in there and tame the lion and you're going to come up with good results.

I have never worn the HANS device. I don't like to have anything, even my radio wire, catch hold on my head. I move a lot in the car – lean into the corners. I feel like I probably won't like it but I'm not going to pass judgment until I try it.

Our team in the 24-hour race finished fourth overall, and second in our class. Dale was happy with what we did.

Dale reminded me of my dad – like the older guys who shoot and ask questions later. He didn't care at all what somebody thinks about him. He had people he liked and people he didn't like. When he had time, not if he was in a good mood or not, to sign autographs, he would. If he didn't have time and people were pushy, he just said "no." He gave all of his time when he could, which was a lot of the time, but he's human like everybody else and needed to have time to just sit and watch the news if he wanted to.

I grew up with my dad and all his old crony motorcycle friends. It brought back a lot of memories by relating with somebody like Dale – tough guys. It was a great experience. He was as much, if not more, a great personality and human and a generous person to everybody he chose to be surrounded by. He was a race car driver. Yeah, he was The Intimidator on the track. What a cool guy off the track. He was always the first one to the track and the last one to leave. For somebody who has been racing as long as he has, big sports figures like that, they sometimes get to the point where they're making their money and doing it because they have to. Not Dale, he still loved it. He loved driving that race car. He thought it was the greatest thing on the planet.

I think he would have raced the 24 hours race again next year.

Courtesy of IMHF

Early Intimidator

Courtesy of Dan Hughes

Jonah Was Right. It's Hard To Keep A Good Man Down.

Dan Hughes

Co-host on QVC show called "For Race Fans Only"

Dan Hughes wishes viewers had seen a different ending to the show of February 14, 1994 – Valentine's Day. "We've got a live show with Earnhardt. Because of logistics, I couldn't get to Daytona and he couldn't get to Westchester, Pennsylvania where our headquarters are. We worked out a simulcast with Channel 2 in Daytona. Dale is in the studio there. I'm home. I close by saying, "Dale, we appreciate you taking time to be part of the program. Good luck at Daytona, and good night. Then I thought, "Wait a minute, it's Valentine's Day." I said, "We've been plugging your sponsors all night, don't you want to plug your wife?" On the air! I was shooting for a Valentine's Day opportunity for Dale to say hello to his wife. I thought, "If Dale doesn't kill me, Teresa will." There was a painfully long pause. Dale said something to the effect of, "Teresa, I love you. I'll see you soon." I saw my career going down in flames. As soon as the show ended, I called the studio in Daytona, and Don Hawk, who was Earnhardt's business manager picked up the phone. I said, "I did not mean to say it that way." He said, "Dale won't talk to you." Then I hear Dale laughing in the background.

Here, I'm supposed to be this professional guy. It turned out to be, for me, by far, the biggest example of just feeling like a heel. It was never intended in any way to be negative. I have so much respect for who Dale was on the track, off the track, the type of guy he is. It was just one of those things where my intentions were good, and I appreciated the Earnhardts having a great sense of humor about it. I thought, "Oh my God, what have I done?"

We had fifty-two minutes each show, and I talked about thirty seconds. If you add it up real quick, and most people aren't aware of this, as far as live TV interview time, Dale spent more time sitting next to me and talking than he did to anybody else on any other network. We're always live. You get an interview that's maybe a fifteen second sound bite when they stick the microphone in the window netting before a race, but we would sit for two hours at a time.

I wasn't blessed to be able to say I am in the 'inner circle' of the people he really cared the most about. But we were business associates, and when we did have an opportunity to get together, we always had a ball.

Out of all the people in motor sports, Dale was the individual who gave QVC and Dan Hughes and the vendors who bring all our products in, the credibility that we now have because he always treated me with respect, even when he first met me, and I was still this kid from Indiana.

The reason why they picked me to do the show isn't because I'm the best salesman in the world and it's certainly not 'full head of hair,' because I am exactly what the audience is – I'm a race fan. I've been working in TV for a dozen years, but I'm still not a TV guy. I get a chance to do what everybody who watches our show wants to is to sit down next to Dale Earnhardt and talk to him. The research part of it is work, but my favorite line is, "My job beats working for a living." I always dig in just to find out the facts that I wanted to know. That's one of the reasons why, after working with Dale for over ten years, I did get to know the guy.

Certainly there are people who are much higher up on his list of people, but I got to know a lot more about the guy behind the wheel. It can sound real hokey and real cliché, but I'm a forty-year old guy who has been doing this for a while and pretty firmly entrenched in it. Everybody still has heroes, and in a lot of ways, he was it. The way he conducted his life, there's not too many guys who can wear the white hat and black hat all at the same time. Even people who disliked him still respected him. I really honestly think that Dale had a genuine like for people. Anybody who's had any success at all knows that sometimes the pressures, the schedules, having to do what you do, you don't get a chance to allow yourself the freedom to really talk to people. Because you've always got to do some or be here and there. Sometimes people can be the distraction to keep you from doing what you want to be doing. For an average person, they see that sometimes as being rude or uncaring. That's not what it is at all. It's just trying to stay focused on the job at hand.

When the show, "For Race Fans Only", first began I really thought the show would do well. I figured I can't be the only guy out there who is a race fan who wants to be able to find products that are involved in the sport.

We were at Dover, Delaware and, same scenario, fifty reporters standing around with their little microcassettes and battery packs and microphones, and I was purposely way past that crowd. Dale came out of his trailer, and it's not that he's upset by it, it's just that it's still very much an intrusion. I guess you kind of have to be there to understand that. It's not a dislike for people in any way, shape or form, I don't want to paint the wrong picture, it's just him having things he had to do. He started walking his way toward the car. He was actually walking away from me. He stopped and turned around and waved his arm up saying, "Get over here" to me. So I walked over. He put his hand on my shoulder and said, "You need something?" I said, "Hey, I don't want to bother you. I know you're busy. Would you have a chance to do a sound bite?" He said, "Yeah. Come on." We walked into the garage area, walked past his car to the back of the garage, and he gave me the sound bite. Nothing was really said, but it made me feel like he knew what I was trying to do.

There are a lot of families where one member of the family was a Dale Earnhardt fan, and the other one wasn't. They enjoyed rooting against him probably as much as the guys enjoyed rooting for him. My partner, Tim, was not a 'Dale Earnhardt fan," but it did affect him a lot.

I know Dale well, but I wasn't Dale's best friend. I saw a whole bunch of stuff on TV and in the press after he was gone where everybody was trying to play that part, but I know I wasn't. I was a business associate who got to know the guy very, very well, but there were a lot of people certainly who knew him better than I. What I did get to know is something that I really treasure. It made me feel very special. I know where I stand in the situation. There are others who knew him much better. But I really do feel lucky that I got to know him as well as I did.

The Golden Voice With The Golden Mike.

Eli Gold

Eli Gold has been one of the pre-eminent broadcasters and commentators of NASCAR events for the past quarter century. Gold, who saw The Intimidator's meteoric rise from the beginning, talks about his most memorable encounters with The Man in Black

I'd been broadcasting NASCAR since '76 so I actually predated Dale Earnhardt on the scene and did some work with him, but my first real close encounter with him might have been in '80-'81. It was that range of time, and was a time in his career where he did not need my help in turning the fans against him. He was getting booed and was not a fan favorite at that point. He was brash in his off-track activity. He was good. He was beating some of the proven veterans. He was a young champion. There were just some things that had gone on out on the race track that did not endear him to the fans.

At Pocono, I can't remember the year, Dale was driving either for Rod Osterlund or the Wrangler car. To this day in my office, and it's been there for the last fifteen years, is the whole right front fender assembly of his blue and yellow car. At Pocono, he got into this hellacious accident with Tim Richmond. They're going down the main straightaway heading into turn one. Pocono is a triangular race track. The front straightaway is the longest single straightaway in all of NASCAR. The front stretch is wider and longer than any other straightaway that we have – Talladega, Daytona. You can land a 747 on the front straightaway at Pocono. It's darn near a mile long. I'm broadcasting on a wooden tower outside of the apex of turn number one – a very, very precarious perch now that we think about it. In those days, it was a great seat. Here come Earnhardt and

Richmond down the front straightaway. They get crossed up somehow, and both cars start flipping wildly. They are barrel-rolling into turn number one. By the mere geometry of the way the track is shaped as a triangle, Richmond's car gets clipped, then it kind of goes off toward the side but Earnhardt's car is flipping right toward me. He's spinning and flipping right toward this wooden tower on which I'm standing. It actually does hit the tower, but thankfully I survived, and the tower survived, and Dale survived. But he was banged up fairly significantly. It was a very scary moment. Shrapnel was going everywhere – sheet metal was flying off the car as it was barrel-rolling. Hence, I went into the woods behind the turn and retrieved that right front fender assembly that now is in my office. I figured – what the heck, the boy about took me out.

Everytime we went back to Pocono thereafter, until I moved into the anchor booth, I was out there on that same perch. On the pace lap, people didn't know this, as Dale came by at whatever speed they were doing, he'd kind of get down around the roll cage because the angle was such he had to kind of gyrate a little bit and he would wave to me standing in that wooden platform as he went by. I would lean down and kind of wave to him as he went by. It was our little thing like – "All right, Dale, you don't come into the broadcast booth here anymore, and I promise never to climb into your car." It was just kind of our own little, "Hey, I see you're still there, and I'm glad you're alive and well."

After Dale had made a special effort for a young boy who had a fatal illness, I go to the race track that weekend wherever it was we were. I went up to Dale and thanked him for calling the kid and said, "I understand you sent him a nice 'care' package." He said, "Yeah, glad to do it, happy to do it. But do me a favor." I said, "What's that?" "Don't say anything about it." I said, "What do you mean?" He said, "I don't do that for any reason just to get PR. We think we've got problems. This kid was a young boy, and he's dying." He was afraid that if there was a lull in the race and I was in the anchor booth, I might have said, "Hey, you know what happened this week?" And that I would tell the story. He said, "I didn't do that for publicity. I'd appreciate your not saying it." I'm sure now the family wouldn't mind my telling the story, but at the time Dale did not want that publicized. It was just something he did.

That was just one kid. You have to wonder through all these years how many times he has done that for other people, and they, too, are just sitting on the story saying, "He didn't want to talk about it."

Another thing was more personal for my family. Even though I never allowed myself to be a fan of any one driver, per se. You know I like them all, get along well, and have a great relationship. But my wife, Claudette, is a big Earnhardt fan. When I'm gone on the weekend to the races, she'll hang an Earnhardt flag outside the house. She just always liked Dale. Whenever she'd see Dale at the race track, he'd always come up and give her a hug – or throw an ice cube at her, or whatever. Just playful stuff.

I don't even know if we respect how much of an influence he was. You knew it, but sometimes you wonder, within our own little cocoon of racing fans and racing followers, you certainly appreciate it. But did you ever expect that World News Tonight would dedicate segments to Earnhardt when he passed away. Did you ever expect to hear the name Earnhardt come through the lips of Peter Jennings? I didn't. Could you ever have imagined this man being on the covers of Time, Newsweek, and SI in the same week? We all knew he was influential within our own sphere of life, but I don't know if I ever totally grasped the total influence that apparently he does have and has had on mainline Americana.

It took him seventeen tries to win his Daytona 500. But I will tell you that by that time, I personally had broadcast hundreds and hundreds, if not a thousand NASCAR events, in all different NASCAR divisions, and when came down pit road, and everybody is running out there and shaking hands, I got choked up. I'm kind of a softie at heart, but I'd seen most everything come down the pike since 1976 when I did my first broadcast, and I've seen a lot of stuff, a lot of experiences. You just felt so good for the man. You imagine that you know what he's feeling.

I did not appreciate the gravity of the moment when the accident happened, the second it happened. I went from talking about the lead back to that. You know it's interesting, to this moment, I have not listened to the tape. I don't know exactly what I said, but I do remember vaguely: "Earnhardt and Schrader go up the bank and into the wall, meanwhile coming off turn four. . . . " – I mean I went right back to the lead, 'cause that's where the story was. I don't think the accident was any more severe, visually, than seemingly hundreds of others that you've seen – that I've seen since the middle seventies. I guess what tipped me off first to the problem was when Schrader walked over to the car, peered in, and then began waving for the safety crew to get over there in a hurry. I realized at that point that something was amiss. Obviously the more time they spent out there, the more concerned we all became. But at a quick glance it was just another racing accident, and I went right back to talking about the battle for the lead. I can't say that at that instant I realized anything was significantly wrong.

It's tough to put it all in focus. We're missing a friend. You miss the nice guy. You expect to see him walk in. He's just not walking in. I will find myself to this day, sitting in an airplane, or wherever I am, and just find myself shaking my head. My mind will drift to Dale Earnhardt.

I guess I always feel these guys are invincible. I know they're not. I'm a smart human. I just always felt he was invincible. Pick a person in your life that you've worked with closely since the late seventies, and if all of a sudden that person is gone, then there is a void there. It's not just his competitiveness, or his ability, it's just everything – just his being there.

It's weird. He was my guest on our NASCAR Live Talk Show on the Tuesday prior.

We did the show from Daytona. It was a great show because the guest lineup was Dale Earnhardt, Michael Waltrip, Jeff Gordon, Bobby Labonte – we had really a strong show. It was the Tuesday before the 500, and he came into the studio wearing blue jeans with a baseball hat on. He was joking around with Jeff Gordon off the air. Dale had run this past February the Rolex 24 – that's the twenty-four hours of Daytona. He was tooling around Daytona in this yellow Corvette – a beautiful competition yellow Corvette convertible. We were sitting in the studio at the time on a commercial break. I said, "Where'd you get that 'vette from?" He said that was part of the deal for driving in the Rolex 24. If you drive for the Corvette team, which he did, they give you the use of that vehicle for a short while. Jeff Gordon said, "Man, I need to drive in that race next year. That's a pretty good deal. I'm driving around in this Monte Carlo, and you're driving around in this." Dale said, "Well, I'm Dale Earnhardt. You're only Jeff Gordon." He was smiling the whole time.

The thing I loved about Dale was the way he grew into his celebrity. He didn't take himself too seriously, or if he did, he kept it hidden. It would not be unusual to go up to his farm, and there he is throwing bales of hay around. He was a celebrity, yes, but he was not too big ever to re-member where he came from and to work on his farm – sometimes the time demands were difficult, but he'd get out there on his tractor and be working and doing and riding around. He was just plain old Dale, who happened to be a world-renowned athlete super star, multi-millionaire. But he was still plain old Dale and that was, I think, what was so very wonderful about him. He was still just old Dale. He had financial security and was still a nice old guy.

It seemed he had a special relationship with Teresa. They seemed to be a very dedicated couple. I know Teresa, and we have done stuff to-gether over the years, but I always ask all the drivers – how's the family, how's the kids, is anybody sick, et cetera? But I never really – that was their private life and I didn't really enter into that much.

Then Chet Said To Cosell, "Level With Me Howard, Or I'll Pull The Rug Right Out From Over You."

Chet Coppock

Chicago-based Chet Coppock is regarded by many as the Number One Sports Talk radio host in America. He is heard on The Sporting News Radio Network.

What always got to me about Earnhardt is the towering effect he had on people. He is the kind of guy who basically told the establishment, "Shove it. I'm going to do it my way. I am The Intimidator." Earnhardt was never the kind of guy who I thought was going to wind up on a cover of Gentleman's Quarterly, yet there was something intrinsic about his appeal to women. The last thing you expect to see is a babe from Brooklyn wearing a Dale Earnhardt jacket. You would see this.

We got confirmation of Dale Earnhardt's death just as I went on the air on the new Sporting News Radio Network. So, really, the whole scope of your program changes. Guests are cancelled. You're zipping down to Ned Jarrett, down to the kid from Fox who does the race blow-by-blow. The one thing I did not deal with which I think becomes cliché-predictable is that Dale would have wanted it no other way. The fact is that's crazy – ridiculous. Dale Earnhardt did not want to die in a race car. He was enjoying life too much to die so young. I was frankly amazed, really taken aback, at the enormity of what he meant. When I woke up the following day and read the Sun Times, Tribune, USA Today, hopped online, I began to realize this guy was arguably just a notch below what you would call the Tiger Woods, Michael Jordan plateau.

I loved this about Dale. You looked at his eyes and beneath the cold steel and the twinkle, you knew there was a guy there who was saying to himself, "Ain't no authority gonna knock this boy down." We all want to defy authority – take the suits and kick them in the butt. Earnhardt did it. He won, and won. If you stop and think about it, he may be our last really, really great people's champion. Is it Sammy Sosa? A-Rod? Forget about it. Troy Aikman? Terrell Davis? No. Allen Iverson? Of course not. Dale Earnhardt, in some respects, was a closing chapter – he really was.

Courtesy of IMHF

The "Winston Select" Win

There Are No Rest Areas On The Highway To Success

Steve Byrnes

Steve Byrnes, the host of Totally NASCAR, became a confi-dante of Dale Earnhardt. Byrnes hunted with Earnhardt and was chosen by him to produce a tape of his life story. The tape was hosted by Neil Bonnett. When Bonnett died in a crash during testing, the tape was never released.

Dale Earnhardt felt he was unfairly portrayed as a reckless driver. Other drivers knew if they saw that black car behind them, he was coming. When you saw Dale Earnhardt in the rear view mirror, you knew he was going to make a move. It wasn't a matter of 'if he was' it was a matter of 'when he was.'

The best interview I ever did with him was while he was baling hay. He was sweating, wiping his brow. He was the first guy I ever heard refer to anybody else as a racer. If he called somebody a racer, that meant that he respected them.

When Neil Bonnett died, a part of Dale died. Watching them to-gether was like – I hate a cliché – but they were soul mates. They rarely talked about racing. It was: Who could catch the biggest bass? Who could get up earliest and be out in the field? They had done more by six a.m. than most people do all day. Earnhardt would get on his bulldozer and knock down trees, or plant crops, tend to his animals. They didn't analyze life; they just attacked it. They were very, very similar. I think that's why they liked each other.

I talked to him in Daytona a couple of days before the accident. My wife and I had been in the Bahamas, and went into a small coffee shop. This nice old man said, "What do you guys do?" "Well, we work at NASCAR." He said, "Oh, do you know Earnhardt?" We said, "Sure," thinking that was the only driver he's ever heard of. But no, he knew

Earnhardt because Earnhardt had his boat down there at times. I mentioned that to Dale at Daytona. He goes, "Oh yeah, I know Captain Forty."

The week of his death, Dale told Darrell Waltrip, "I'm the luckiest guy in the world. I've had a great career – got a great wife – a great family. I'm a guy who has it all." When he was younger and lacking funds, he'd scrape and do anything he could to get by to race, and I really feel like even though he had all the accoutrements of wealth and fame, all the stuff around him changed but didn't change him. I think he felt at peace and felt comfortable with who he was as a person.

Courtesy of IMHF

Ralph Earnhardt's boys–Dale, Danny, Randy in front of one of Dad's early cars.

The Biggest Earnhardt Fan In Baja, Minnesota

Mike Lee

Mike is the biggest Dale Earnhardt fan in his hometown of Mason City, Iowa. Now living in Des Moines, he made many sacrifices to see Earnhardt race. His story is but one of a million Earnhardt fans could tell.

I went back to Daytona for this year's 500. I listened to Dale and his crew off and on pretty much throughout the entire race, especially after the wreck involving Tony Stewart and seventeen other cars, which happened at around lap 178. They were under a caution flag and Dale was talking. First of all, he went off on a tirade with his crew chief and crew – Dale has always been pretty outspoken about what he felt personally with NASCAR rules and restrictor plates and the packages that they dealt to them. He raced it, but he definitely let people know what he thought of it. He went on a tear about how it was a bomb waiting to go off – a time bomb. He said he knew something like this big accident would happen. He got it out of his system.

They went back to racing and then pretty much after he got back into that green-flag racing, I heard him talking back and forth with his crew. Dale was competing and he was aggressive and everything, but willing to give a little bit more for his teammates, his son, the cars that he owned. He promised Michael Waltrip a win if he would come on board with him. Michael Waltrip had suffered and struggled and hadn't really been provided with very good equipment prior to coming on board with Dale Earnhardt, Inc. I don't know if he gave everything he could to make good on that promise to him but he did get the win in Dale Earnhardt's last race.

There was no conversation on the scanner at the time of his accident. I did not hear any impact noises or anything at the time of impact. I did hear his teammates, his crew calling to him asking, "Dale, if you're okay, say something to us. We want to hear from you. Let us know you're okay." No response from him at all.

I saw the accident. I didn't think that it was a lethal impact. I thought that it was probably – he might be hurt – I've seen so many accidents where it looks so spectacular and the people just basically walk away from them with just minor injuries. I thought well maybe he's hurt a little bit. Maybe he got shook up a little bit and he's not responding. Maybe it just damaged his radio, and he couldn't respond or couldn't hear them calling to him. I didn't anticipate that it was lethal, with the outcome the way it was. I was concerned when I saw Kenny Schrader go up to the car and look in and was immediately pretty emphatical about getting some help to Dale Earnhardt's car. Kenny Schrader was the one who impacted him as he hit the wall, and their cars came to rest right near each other in the grass area just outside of turn four.

I was really concerned about the covering up of his car as quickly as they did. One of the other fans in the stands, though, indicated to me that was kind of an Earnhardt trait, which I hadn't noticed before. I was taking his word for it that Earnhardt did not like for people to see his car banged up, in that kind of a condition.

I didn't sense that it was that bad – that he would die. I sensed that he was hurt. The crowd was somber – the crowd, myself, more so that you would normally see after the Daytona 500. We decided we were going to go ahead and try to get back to my aunt and uncle's house in Daytona where we were staying. We hoped maybe they had heard additional word over the media by the time we would get there. Probably within an hour and fifteen minutes after the end of the race we got back to their house. I was in the bathroom getting ready to shower when my father yelled in to me that it was unofficial but it was announced that Dale had died in the crash

We were planning to leave Daytona about 4 or 5 a.m. on Monday following the race. After the word of Dale's death, I told my Dad, "There's no way I can leave now. I have to go back to the track." First, we tried to get a newspaper of his death to bring back. This was difficult because people were stealing papers off of people's doorsteps and out of their driveways in Daytona. We stopped at every store, every newspaper machine we could find, and they were all out. I ended up going directly to the paper to get a copy.

I went to the race in Las Vegas about a month after Dale died. I've been working hard and finally got the opportunity to get pit passes. My nephew called me during 'Speed Week' while I was down in Daytona and told me they were secured for Vegas. I had just purchased, before I left for

Daytona, a special hand drawing – pencil drawing, of Dale Earnhardt in his car. I had anticipated getting to meet him for the first time and hopefully get his autograph – actually get to meet my hero. I had a great time. I really am glad I finally got to go into the pits and experience it. There was something missing – a lot missing for me because Dale wasn't there.

In Iowa, it's tough to build yourself into a race fan because we are fairly isolated from the NASCAR circuit community – being able to go to the races. We are starting to get a couple of races now into the Midwest— this year Kansas City and Chicago. It was quite difficult for me to even anticipate getting to a race up until just a couple of years ago when I started to be able to do it. I don't make much money – about twenty five thousand dollars a year, and I think last year I probably spent almost half my income on going to different kinds of races, whether it was NASCAR, World of Outlaws, drag races. Between going to the races and buying race collectibles, apparel, things like that, I actually moved back in with my parents after living out of the house for ten years. A lot of the reason was so that I could do things like this. I'm almost 34 years old.

It's easy for people to try to make fun of a 33-year old man who lives with his parents, but I can usually rest assured that I'm doing more things that I enjoy than those people who are trying to say that I'm less than they are for living with my parents. Actually, I couldn't have better roommates than they are so. . . .

I saw Richard Childress in Vegas. I asked him to autograph a photo of Dale's car that I took personally in Daytona. He did and was a very accommodating person. I told him I was thinking about him, and the family and the whole team and everything. When I was showing that photo to him, one of the marketing people who had put together an advertising package for Sonic on his car actually approached me to see if they could have a copy of that picture, too. It was their first year with putting the package together on his car and no one anticipated that this possibly would be an outcome and they didn't have any photos from the fans' perspective.

I keep trying to think what are all the good things coming up, if any. I'm a strong believer in fate. I don't know necessarily if there are any good things that will come of it but I hope that there is.

If They Ain't Rubbin', They Ain't Racin'

Bob Latford

After attending high school in Daytona Beach and then going into the army in the early 1950s, Bob Latford was hired by Bill France, Sr. to work in the publicity department of the Daytona International Speedway. He later worked at the Atlanta Motor Speedway, then at the Charlotte Motor Speedway. While there in 1975, he designed the points system still used to determine the Winston Cup driving championship.

Latford, like so many racing historians, places Dale Earnhardt at the top of the racing hierarchy.

When Dale first came into racing in '75, he was another of the second-generation of drivers coming into the sport. He was following his dad, a guy with a lot of talent on the local dirt tracks in North Carolina. The first time he ever ran on a big track was in the early '70s, when he drove one of Neil Castle's cars in a Sportsman's race, and like so many of the good ones, he was able to get more out of the car than should have been gotten. You see that with the young guys who come in who really have the ability. He'd drive a car that had been running in the back of the pack and drive it in the front half, and he showed he could do that, and it impressed people.

Dale had the wherewithal to be able to win, and he had the ability. He served his apprenticeship on dirt tracks and driving the secondary cars, and he had honed those skills, which were innate, which you can see by the accelerated rate by which he went through the procedure. He came up and became a winner.

It was the evolution of the Childress team and the evolution of Earnhardt, because under Moore, he had the old school rigid taskmaster who helped him learn how to compete on the big tracks, and Childress was evolving his team, patterning it more after Junior Johnson's operation, which is what he continues to do. That was the guide he set up because it was so successful.

The one common bond between Dale and Richard Childress was both grew up poor. Childress' first association with racing was selling peanuts in the grandstand of Bowman-Gray Stadium in Winston-Salem during the modified races over there, and Earnhardt was banging on the dirt tracks. They were fulltime, dedicated racers, and most of the successful teams have been that way.

Dale won a lot of victories over the years, and looking back I'd say his most spectacular was the one at Talladega last year (2000), where he came out of nowhere to win. Part of theory, and I meant to ask Dale about it but never did, was not the fact that he could 'see the air' in those tight races, but because of the open-faced helmet he could feel it. He could feel the change of pressure on his skin, which with a full-face, he wouldn't have been able to do.

Of course, the most sentimental victory was the one at the Daytona 500. He had come so close so many times. He had led virtually all but seven laps of the Daytona 500s. Lap 1, 2, 3, 4, lap 87, lap 167, but the one he never led was lap 200. He had led lap 199, 198, 197 and the 500 was about the only thing at Daytona he had not won that he had ever tried. And there was a great deal of sentiment because everybody appreciated how good he was and how close he had come, and to see him be the bridesmaid that many times and never get to the altar, and then all of a sudden, he wins – the reception and response of the other crews is what made it so special.

And not only was Dale a great racer, he was a brilliant businessman. He's the one as much as anyone who, with Don Hawk, pioneered the whole souvenir industry. Look what he made on the race track – he's won more money than anyone in the history of racing – but it pales in comparison to what he made on his souvenirs.

In addition to the money he made, Dale had a wonderful image, and Joe Whitlock had a great deal to do with that, because he was with Wrangler, and he came up with The Intimidator name and the 'One Tough Customer' slogan.

Dale will certainly be missed

The parallel I tell people, because many fans were not involved with the sport back in the 60s, was to when Fireball Roberts died. Fireball was our biggest name. He was the magic name people came to see. People who didn't even follow racing knew Fireball Roberts, and this is much the same thing. Dale was THE big name of the sport, and suddenly he's been taken away.

But looking forward, the racing is still competitive and good. This year, we had more competitive events than we had last year when he was out there. There are times when they keep bringing it up, pumping it up, mostly to make money. They are having the Auto Fair here at the Speedway and right now they have a special Earnhardt commemorative area with some of the cars, and it's been played very heavily in their advertising, even though the Earnhardt family won't get anything out of it. You hate to see that aspect of it, but I think dignified respect too is paying to his contributions and the talent that he was.

I'd say my most vivid memory of Dale is that wrinkled smile of his. Under the mustache there was the twinkle in the eye that just said, 'Hey, there's mischief coming.'

It's Hard To Cheer With A Broken Heart

Dick Berggren

Berggren has been a commentator and color man for ESPN, CBS and now Fox.

You have to realize that later in his career Dale went entire seasons without crashing or getting a DNF. He became masterful at avoiding trouble, but when he got into it, it was big.

With Fox television, every time the Winston Cup cars moved, we had a television show. We did virtually all the practices live, and you always want to get Earnhardt, because Earnhardt is always the story, especially at Daytona. One day after practice, I went in to the garage and pointed to my microphone, which is what I do when I'm asking for an interview. Earnhardt just looked at me, and with his four fingers, he motioned. 'Go away, little boy.' I slumped off and went around the car and started to go out the back of the garage, and I said into my microphone to the control room, "Earnhardt doesn't want to talk now." I just got done saying that and all of a sudden this very strong hand grabs my elbow, and it's Earnhardt. He has this s_ _t-eating grin on his face. He says, "How about now?"

Dale Earnhardt was absolutely the best stock car racer I've ever seen, and I've been following this sport for fifty years. He could do things with cars others would never attempt, and if they did, they couldn't successfully do it.

I do believe he could feel air. I do believe he could smell openings. He put cars in places other people couldn't. He had a unique technique for loosening the car up in front of him so he could execute a pass, but not spin the guy out so he could avoid the penalty. No one could do things like that as well as he could do them.

He was an extraordinarily positive influence for the sport - a guy who came up from nothing. What he made of himself, he did himself. He didn't just do it driving race cars. Other people have driven race cars and not created the huge empire he did. He's just an amazing personality and a role model for everyone else who says, "Gee, I don't have anything. I don't even have a good education. What can I possibly do with my life?" And I say to anybody who says this, "Look at Dale Earnhardt .He was a success at everything he attempted - a wonderful role model."

All the world knows Dale Earnhardt, and I don't think there has ever been a racing driver who has had that kind of recognition or that kind of awareness on the part of the American public. Certainly, when A. J. Foyt, Mario Andretti and Richard Petty were in their heyday, there was not television or newspaper coverage like there is now. And Richard Petty was a great sports icon, but Dale Earnhardt was the greatest icon the motor sports world has ever seen.

We can get excited on Sunday afternoon and cheer for our favorite and boo for the guy we dislike, but the guy who was the shining star, the guy who moved more fans than anybody else, is gone.

THE FINISH LINE

Number 3 proved that there is no expiration date on dreams. Not only was he a winner, he turned into a really neat guy. Thanks for the dance, Dale.

ML   11/04